FOUR VOICES

How They Affect Our Mind

How to Overcome Self-destructive Voices and Hear the Nurturing Voice of God

Yong Hui V. McDonald

FOUR VOICES, HOW THEY AFFECT OUR MIND
How to Overcome Self-destructive Voices and Hear the Nurturing Voice of God

Books, audio books, DVDs written and produced by Yong Hui V. McDonald are also available. To purchase, contact www.griefpathway.com or email at griefpwv@gmail.com or order by phone: 1-800-booklog, 1-800-266-5564. GriefPathway Ventures, LLC, P.O. Box 220, Brighton, CO 80601. Adora Productions is an imprint of the GriefPathway Ventures, LLC.

Published by Adora Productions
Printed in the United States of America
ISBN: 978-1-935791-02-7

Cover Design by Lynette McClain
McClain Productions
www.mcclainproductions
Cover Art & Design Copyright © 2011 Adora Productions
First Printing: November 2011

1. Destructive Voices 2. How to Listen to God's Voice
3. Spiritual Healing 4. Inspirational

CONTENTS

DEDICATION
ACKNOWLEDGMENTS

ACKNOWLEDGMENTS

My mother prays for me and my ministry day and night. I believe because of her prayers, God has blessed me and my ministry beyond my imagination. She has been my cheerleader and I thank God for her. I am also deeply indebted to my wonderful husband, Keith, who died in a car accident in July 2008 and is with the Lord. Keith brought healing in my heart and helped my ministry preparation more than anyone else I've ever met. I also thank my beautiful children. I pray that God will bless them beyond their imagination in all areas of life.

My gratitude to all the people who have contributed their stories for this book and the following ACDF saints: Burnie and Richard Cordova drawings. The following saints helped me edit this book: Juanita Adams, Dee Anderson, Billy bob Bramscher, Don Burough, Cody Bushman, Francesca Cayou, Desuray Cisneross, Kathleen W. Cooper, Mary Diubaldo, Patricia Dawson, James Escalante, Rita Finney, Robert Garcia, Felonis Hernandez, Richard Irwin, Cheryl Killion, Heather Lopez, Paul Reaves, Jennifer Richardson, Amber Roesch, Tina Roberts, Lupe Rubio, Jessany Unrein-Russom, Jennifer Spade, Juanita Tamayo, Rodney Thurber, Cannon Tubb, Lakiesha Vigil, Mary Voogt, Mary Matteo, Robie Sothman, Gloria Vera, Mireya Vizcarra, Bernadette Warling, Phyllis Wells, and Georgette Wires. The following volunteers helped me with editing: Cassie Foust, Janet Lysco, Amy Penn, and Glenda Yeisley. Thank you for all your hard work and God bless you.

Finally, I give glory to Jesus. Without Him, this book could not have been written.

DEDICATION

I dedicate this book to our Heavenly Father, our Lord Jesus, the Holy Spirit, and to all those who are in need of healing from self-destructive voices and want to learn to listen to the voice of God.

Chapter 1

How Did This Book Come About?

Why the book *Four Voices*? After I started my prison ministry in 1999, many people asked me how to listen to God's voice. I started writing this book in 2000. However, God directed me to write another book instead. Interestingly, that book was about how God spoke to me and it was republished as *I Was The Mountain*.

At the time I couldn't understand why He didn't let me finish this book. In 2011, about eleven years later, after I taught so many people how to listen to God's voice, I understood why. I wasn't ready back then. I needed to learn more about listening to God's voice both personally and in the ministry.

Learning to recognize and listen to God's voice is a very important part of my spiritual journey. It changed my life and my walk with the Lord for the better. I am more prepared to deal with life's challenges because I have confidence that God is speaking to me and leading my life and my ministry.

A person who is not able to recognize God's voice is in a dark room and many times is confused. When people finally learn to recognize and hear God's voice, they literally come alive. It changes a person's outlook on life especially when they know that God does care and will guide them by speaking to them.

Can we learn how to listen to the voice of God? Yes, from my personal and ministry experiences, I learned that anyone can learn how to listen to the voice of

God. Listening to God's voice is a skill we can learn. It may take time but as long as a person is willing to learn, wait and listen, eventually they will recognize and hear His voice.

I heard from many people that they want to hear God's voice but they haven't heard anything. Why do people have a difficult time hearing God's voice? As I was teaching others how to listen to God, it became clear to me that there are three major reasons why people have a difficult time hearing God's voice.

First, many people do not understand there are different voices they hear in their minds. They have a difficult time recognizing where these voices are coming from. In fact, many people suffer from hearing bad voices and they are tormented and troubled and do not know how to stop these voices. This book will guide those who suffer from bad voices to learn how to let go of their bad voices and recognize God's voice.

Second, many people don't understand that God has many languages and He can speak to us in many different ways.

Third, many people's minds are too busy with other things and they do not take the time to quiet their mind and listen in silence to hear God's voice.

I pray that you will gain an understanding of the different voices, learn to control your thoughts and also to hear the voice of the Lord who speaks to us in many ways.

Chapter 2

Four Voices

People generally believe that their thoughts are their own creation and that the "voices" carrying the thoughts are also self-made. That's not true. It's critical to understand the origin of the voices and thoughts if we want to live a peaceful and productive life. If we don't understand the origin of the voices or thoughts, we can develop wrong perceptions and attitudes toward ourselves and others which will eventually affect our actions and our lives and the lives of those around us.

Drawing "Different Voices" by Burnie

There are four voices we hear in our mind:
(1) Our voice
(2) Other peoples' voices
(3) Bad voices — destructive, negative
(4) Good voices — productive, positive

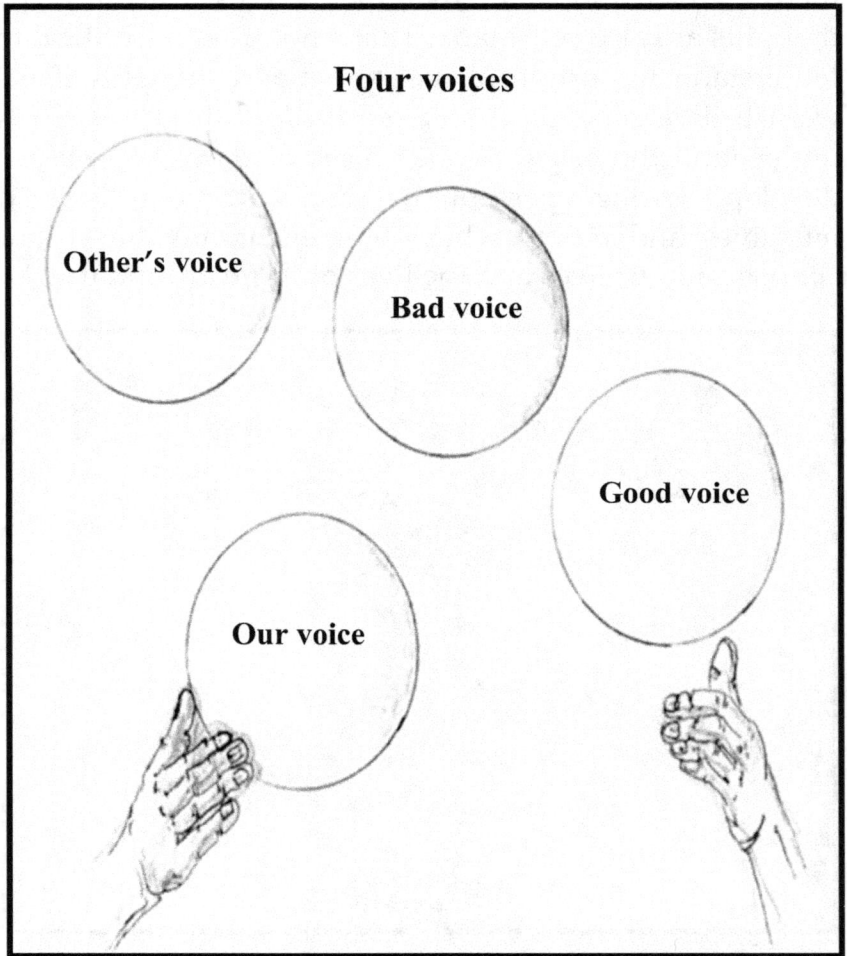

Four voices

Other's voice

Bad voice

Good voice

Our voice

Drawing "Four Voices" by Burnie

1. Our voices

Our voices are good or bad thoughts depending on what we focus on. We are the final decision maker of our thoughts. It's called choices. We choose every day on which voice we want to accept and which one we want to reject.

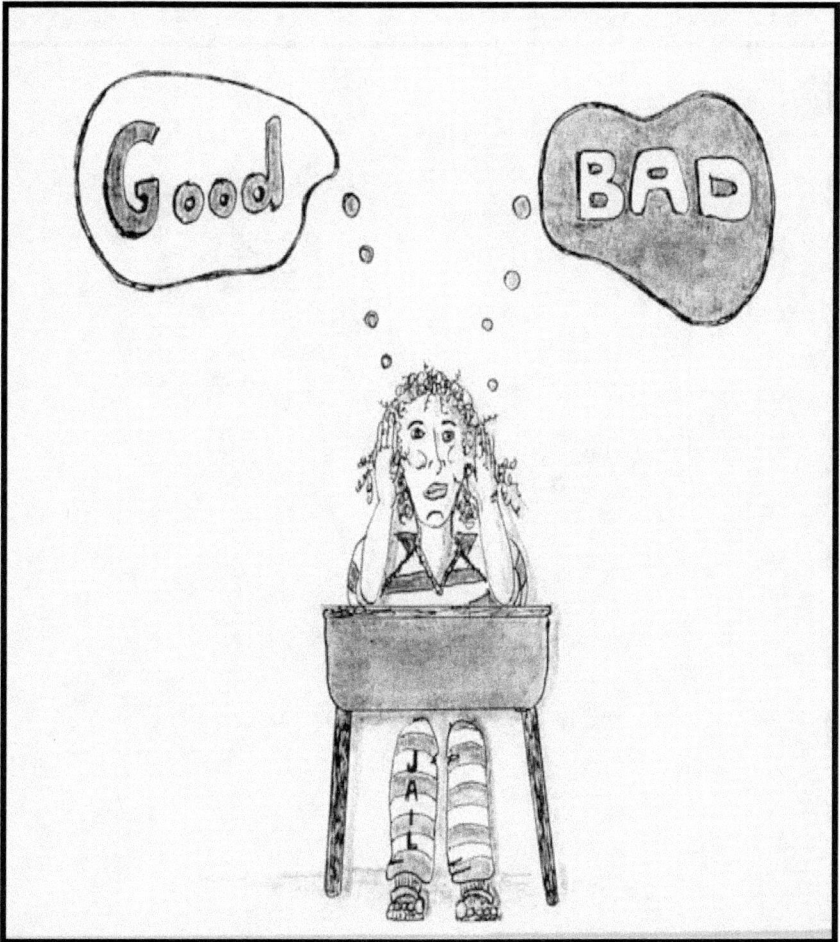

Drawing "Our Voices" by Burnie

2. The voices of other people

Other peoples' voices are what other people say or what we read and hear about others in our minds. These voices can be good or bad. Many times these voices in our minds start outside when others make comments about us. Then the message starts replaying over-and-over in our minds.

Drawing "Other People's Voices" by Burnie

3. Bad voices

The bad voices that come to our minds are not good and they keep playing in our minds even when we try to let it go. Some just call them bad thoughts and some call them the devil's voice, depending on your understanding of the voice. These voices are hurtful and suggest that we do something bad to ourselves and to others. We can be in turmoil if we don't know how to resist them.

Drawing "Bad Voices" by Burnie

4. Good voices

The good voices are voices and thoughts that come to our mind, or are audible, but they are not coming from people. It's coming from a good spirit which some call the "Holy Spirit" and some call them angel voices or their conscience. These voices are always good, encouraging and directing us to live a good life. They tell us to take a good path and avoid doing bad things so that we don't get into trouble.

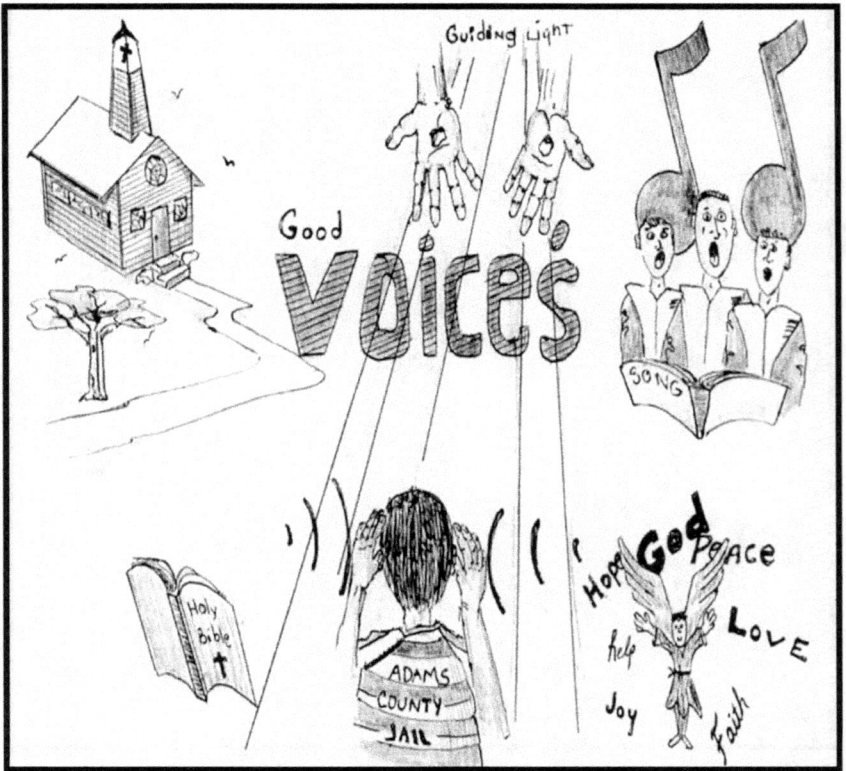

Drawing "Good Voices" by Burnie

5. What do good voices and bad voices do?

We make choices everyday influenced by good voices and bad voices. Many people struggle, however, unable to tell the difference between the voices. They have a difficult time deciding which voice to trust. It's very important to recognize where these voices are coming from so we can resist bad voices, accept good voices and make the right decisions.

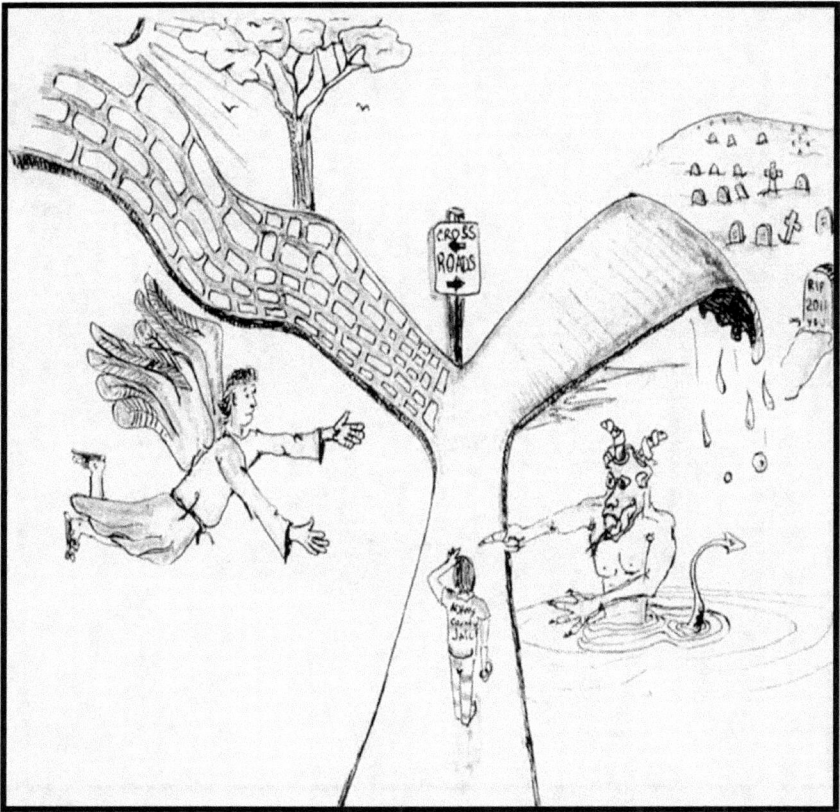

Drawing "Good and Bad Voices" by Burnie

6. Bad voices and choices

Bad voices try to make us choose the path that will cause us to get into trouble, turmoil and pain. We need to learn to resist these voices. If we choose to listen to bad voices, we end up hurting ourselves and others.

Drawing "Bad Voices and Choices" by Burnie

7. Good voices and choices

Good voices help us take the right path so we can have peace and help ourselves and others have a better life. God's voice is the "good voice" and He wants to help us take the right path.

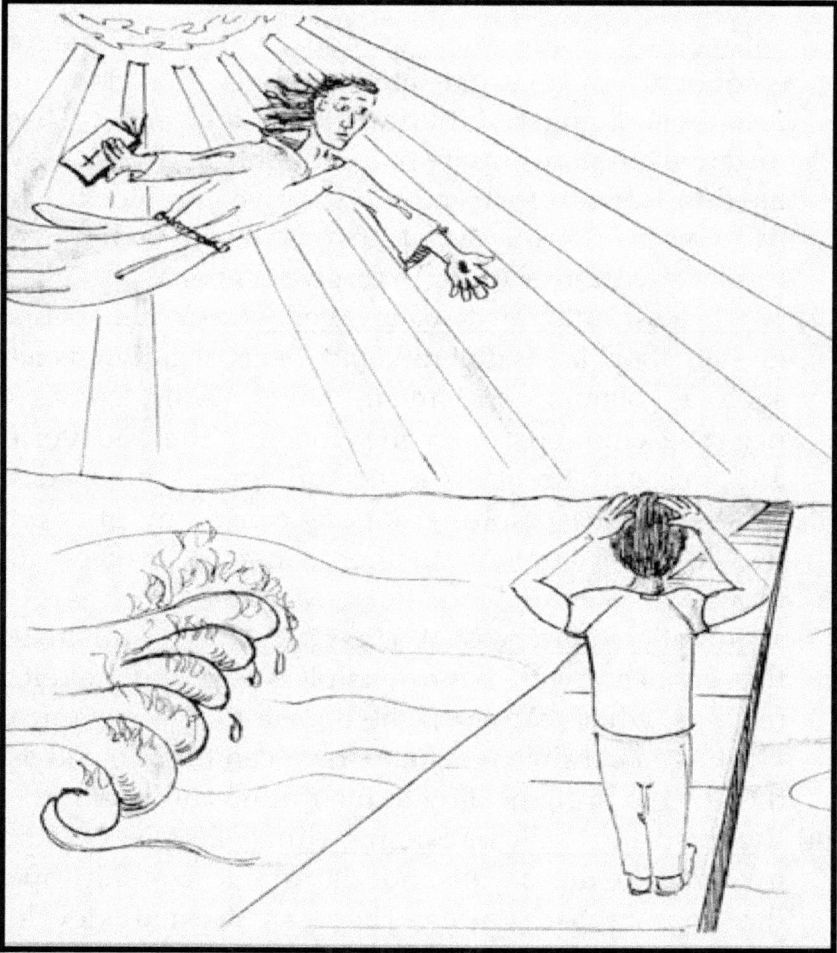

Drawing "Good Voices and Choices" by Burnie

Chapter 3

When Do We Hear Bad Voices?

People tend to hear more bad and negative voices when they experience the following:

(1) <u>Difficulties in life such as abuse</u>: Physical, mental, emotional and sexual abuse opens the door for resentment, anger, bitterness, fear and hate. These negative emotions invite bad thoughts and voices. We have to learn to forgive others so we can block these bad voices. In some cases, a person has to be removed from a situation in order to forgive others.

(2) <u>Grief, loss, and death of a loved one</u>: When people grieve, they are vulnerable to hear negative voices such as blame, resentment, anger, guilt, etc. Any negative emotions open the door for the bad voices and this can occur in grief and loss. You need to process all the painful emotions caused by grief and loss in order for you to ignore the bad voices and thoughts.

(3) <u>Traumatic experiences</u>: When a person is traumatized, this creates anger, blame, helplessness and hopeless feelings, which can open the door for negative voices. Healing is possible when a person can forgive and ask the Lord to bring healing to their minds and hearts.

(4) <u>Involved in a cult or Satanic ritual</u>: People who are involved in the occult and/or Satanic worship open the door to bad voices. They can learn to develop good voices through reading the Bible, praying and

relying on the Lord for healing. They also need to repent of any involvement with the occult and satanic activities and learn to resist bad voices with the Word of God.

(5) Addiction: People who suffer from addictions or addictive lifestyles invite bad voices. Examples of addictions include sex, violence, drugs and alcohol abuse. When people are obsessed with immoral practices or lose control over their thoughts because of substance abuse, that's when bad voices can tell them to do something they would never do when they are sober. Prescription drugs can also affect someone's brain causing vulnerability to bad voices. You have to stop abusing your mind and body through addiction so that you will be able to control your thoughts. You need to ask the Lord for forgiveness and start using your mind and body to glorify the Lord. As you start following the Lord, staying away from any kind of destructive addiction, the bad voices will diminish and you will be able to control your thoughts.

(6) Living in sin: When we live in sin and do things that are not right, we start to hear bad voices telling us how bad we are. Good voices will tell us to change our ways. Bad voices will condemn us. When we fall into sin, bad voices will use that opportunity to wear us down with a heavy heart. We need to repent and change our ways so we will have a clear conscience.

(7) Losing focus: When our hearts are not on loving the Lord, but loving people and things more than God, we open the door for bad voices and we lose focus on listening to the good voices coming from the Lord. We pay the price when we ignore God whether we realize

it or not. Start reading the Bible, praying, following the Lord, and loving God more than people or things. An idle mind and lack of purpose: When people do not have clear goals and a purpose in life, they tend to focus on something they shouldn't and they end up wasting their time and resources on something that is not productive. An idle mind is susceptible to bad voices. Find out how you can serve God by serving others. This will help you focus on positive, not negative things.

(8) Immoral media and video games: Some people spend so much time watching violent shows, immoral shows, and playing violent video games. These activities open the door for bad voices. They need to avoid watching ungodly shows and playing violent video games. They need to read the Bible to hear good voices and pray so they can learn to glorify God and serve others instead of listening to bad voices and thoughts.

(9) Having ungodly people around them: When you associate with people with low moral values, and hold bad conversations, you will be influenced by them. This will open the door for bad voices. Try to spend less time with people who are critical, judgmental, and immoral—especially those who talk badly about others or point at you and say how bad you are. Surround yourself with good people who talk godly talk and have high moral values and say good things about you and others. You need God's discernment to know whom you should be associated with, so ask Him to help you to find godly people who can help you hear good voices.

(10) <u>Anger and an unforgiving heart</u>: When people are filled with anger and do not forgive, they invite bad voices. We need to realize that we all have sinned, yet we are forgiven by God. No one is perfect, but God forgives us when we ask for forgiveness and He has unconditional love for us. Jesus is willing to forgive those who nailed him to the cross and we need to forgive ourselves and others. Resist any bad voices that make you feel miserable. Ask the Lord to help you to see your spiritual condition when you are having a difficult time forgiving others. Ask Jesus to share with you His forgiving heart.

<u>What kind of voices are bad voices?</u>
(1) Voices that tell you that you are useless or worthless and that no one loves you, including God.
(2) Voices that tell you to hurt yourself by giving up, hurting yourself, or tempting you to attempt suicide.
(3) Voices that give people direction on how to hurt themselves or others.
(4) Voices that curse and demoralize people.
(5) Voices that say God caused your problems.
(6) Voices that say God will not answer your prayers, so it's useless to pray.
(7) Voices that say to be angry at God.
(8) Voices that say certain people do not deserve respect and love.
(9) Voices that tell you to hate God and hate others.
(10) Voices that say you cannot quit an addiction.
(11) Voices that tell you that you are a failure and God cannot forgive you.
    The result of following bad voices can be

devastating. How many times have we read in the newspaper that someone committed a crime or suicide while hearing the voices that told them to hurt and kill themselves and others? Therefore, it's critical for us to recognize these bad voices and resist them with the love of God.

Here are some stories of people who have heard bad voices and how they learned to resist them:

Stormi Orton's story: I had a brain aneurysm and became very sick. At the same time my husband was sentenced to ten years in prison. Then my sister passed away and during that time my house burned down. I started to use drugs to self medicate because I couldn't cope with my problems. I got in trouble with the law and lost custody of my children. I felt hopeless and lost faith in God. I didn't pray for over a year nor did I see or speak to my children or family. The devil said, "They don't want you or love you anymore. You are totally worthless." Then one night I heard a voice say, "Pray and ask for forgiveness. God loves you." So, I prayed for over five hours. I told God I had been angry and I blamed Him and thought He didn't love me or care. Otherwise, all these bad things wouldn't have happened. Before all these bad things happened, I was a good person living right. So, I was at a point where I prayed all night for God's will to be done in my life and I called my mother. Well, I had been on the run for over a year and the next day I was arrested. I've been clean ever since.

Francesca Cayou's story: While I was growing up, my siblings told me, "You are not good enough. You are too stupid to get it. You are retarded." How did I get over these voices? I asked myself, "Are these statements true?" My answer was "No." Then I would pray that God would help me to see my accomplishments and to be proud of myself for achieving my goals. Today I say, "I can do it with Jesus."

Ruby Padilla's story: I had an abusive relationship and I felt like my boyfriend was all I needed in life. I had voices telling me that I was worthless. I wasn't thinking of my kids when I was out drinking and depressed. I was suicidal and I felt worthless. I then began to drive home intoxicated on the highway at fast high speeds. I wasn't thinking that I could hurt or kill myself or possibly others. I couldn't even see the road because I was crying. I had a voice telling me I was worthless and I had a vision of wrecking, dying and hurting others in this accident. I was being deceived. Suddenly, I felt the Lord in my heart and I prayed for forgiveness and asked Him to give me peace and get me home safely. I felt peace and safety and then everything negative I had felt was gone. The tears were instantly gone. I was home safe.

Connie Russom's story: I had a run in with the authorities and I remember hearing cussing and rebellious voices. I heard the voice say it did not matter if I was locked away and that God wasn't going to comfort me and that He was the reason why I was being beat up and put in discipline. I remember falling to my knees, screaming to God, "Why?" I cussed and swore to get revenge. I never got out of this stage of torture and crying myself to sleep. The next morning I was transported to

DOC (Department of Corrections) where I found myself in a even darker place, surrounded by demonic people. My healing came when I was put in the Behavioral Program, 23 hour lock down. I knew that all the weight on my shoulders was bringing me to a point where I became weak in my mind and body. I started reading the Bible and watching Joyce Myers in the morning to give me peace, so I would make it through another long day. The Holy Spirit started convicting me when I would do wrong. I did hear the Holy Spirit but just wouldn't obey. In my conviction, I would feel guilty like a little child would feel when they were scolded by their parents. I got tired of feeling alone and being in DOC. I felt it was all just fake to me. I needed something to hope for, to walk with, to trust. I asked to pray with the Chaplain. My prayer was answered and the negative thoughts were removed.

Conclusion

We all have goodness in us so we all have good thoughts and we can also remember good voices from others. The voice that guides you to do good and gives you directions on how to be good, however, comes from the good voice which is from the Lord. The Lord's voice is also the voice of forgiveness.

We can also have bad thoughts and also our thoughts can be affected by what other people do and say. The voices that guide you to do bad things like hurt yourself and others comes from bad spirits. We need to learn how to discern the voices; follow good voices and resist bad voices to find peace and to create peace in our homes and in the community.

Bad voices go against God's values. We should reject any voice that undermines the love of God and His love for us. Any voice that tells us we are worthless, we need to resist.

Chapter 4

How To Resist Bad Voices

Everyone hears bad voices in their minds so we need to learn how to resist them.

1. How can I resist bad voices?

(1) Pray: "Lord Jesus, come, and bless me with your wisdom. Teach me how to resist bad thoughts and voices and to follow your voice, so I may make the right decisions, and live a good, peaceful and godly life."

(2) Read the Bible: Start reading the Bible and meditating on the Scriptures. The Word of God has spiritual power. You will be strengthened as you read the Bible and pray for healing in your mind. Have faith in Jesus and ask him to help you. He will help you to find peace in times of trouble and you may rely on Him. Reject any bad voices and recite the following Scriptures: *"The Spirit of the Lord is on me, because he has anointed me to preach good news to the poor. He has sent me to proclaim freedom for the prisoners and recovery of sight for the blind, to release the oppressed, to proclaim the year of the Lord's favor."* (Luke 4:18-19)

(4) Practice silence: Joan had been tormented since childhood by curse words that would keep repeating over and over again in her mind. She couldn't figure out what she should do to stop that. Nothing helped until she learned how to practice silence. Eventually, she was able to control her thoughts and these voices stopped. Practicing silence is different from having an

idle mind. An idle mind is a wondering mind that invites any voices. When you practice silence, you try to let go of thoughts and clear your mind so you can control your thoughts so you can focus on listening to God. Prayer: "Lord Jesus, speak to me, I am listening."

(5) <u>Forgive</u>: Many people who hear voices have gone through traumatic events in their lives and need healing. As long as you hold on to resentment, anger, bitterness and hatred, you will be opening the door to bad voices. Forgive others and forgive yourself. God values you and forgives you. That's why Jesus died on the cross for our sins. Prayer: "Lord Jesus, thank you for forgiving me. You died on the cross for my sins. I forgive myself and others who have hurt me. I bless those who have hurt me. I pray for others who have hurt me. Heal my wounds and my painful memories and fill my heart with your love, peace, joy and compassion. Help me to have your loving and a forgiving heart, so I can love you as well as others."

(6) <u>Understand the spiritual battle</u>: Fighting with bad voices is a spiritual battle. When you try to resist bad voices and they keep coming back, know that you need more than your strength to win the battle. Find out which area you need to work on from Paul's letter where he gives us clear directions on how to put on the full armor of God. *"Finally, be strong in the Lord and in his mighty power. Put on the full armor of God so that you can take your stand against the devil's schemes. For our struggle is not against flesh and blood, but against the rulers, against the authorities, against the powers of this dark world and against the spiritual forces of evil in the heavenly realms. Therefore put on the full armor of God, so*

that when the day of evil comes, you may be able to stand your ground, and after you have done everything, to stand. Stand firm then, with the belt of truth buckled around your waist, with the breastplate of righteousness in place, and with your feet fitted with the readiness that comes from the gospel of peace. In addition to all this, take up the shield of faith, with which you can extinguish all the flaming arrows of the evil one. Take the helmet of salvation and the sword of the Spirit, which is the word of God. And pray in the Spirit on all occasions with all kinds of prayers and requests. With this in mind, be alert and always keep on praying for all the saints." (Ephesians 6:10-18) Prayer: "Holy Spirit, help me to know which areas I need to work on and in which areas I need to make changes so I can be strong in the Lord and put on the full armor of God so I can have the wisdom and strength to resist the bad voices and serve the Lord." Resist the voice: Whenever you suffer from bad voices, resist the devil by relying on Jesus. You can say, "In the name of Jesus, leave me, I am a child of God."

2. How long will we be hearing bad voices? Can we shut them off completely?

We cannot shut them off completely as long as we live. But we can control how much we hear them by recognizing and resisting them with Jesus' power. Also, we can learn to focus on hearing good voices through spiritual discipline. Jesus gave us the power and authority to drive out demons and that includes resisting bad voices which come from bad spirits. *"When Jesus had called the Twelve together, he gave them power and authority to drive out all demons and to cure diseases" (Luke 9:1)*

3. Why do we even try to resist and fight bad voices if we hear them until we die?

We are given a choice. God gave us a choice from the beginning whether we want to choose to follow the bad voices or the good voices. The consequence of following a bad voice is that we end up doing things we shouldn't do and we live in misery and pain. However, God can forgive us when we ask for forgiveness. Jesus has already won the spiritual battle and we can learn to resist the bad voices through His example.

Chapter 5

Developing Good Voices

Bad voices give us turmoil and good voices give us light in the darkness. They show us which path to avoid and which path to follow so that we can find peace.

Q: Can we control the voices we hear?

Yes, you can with practice. The goal is to gradually hear less and less of the bad voices and to listen more and more to the good voices. How can we do that? The following process can help you develop a habit of listening to good voices and blocking out bad voices.

How to Hear Good Voices

1. Prayer

Praying helps us to focus on God, developing our ability to focus on hearing good voices. God is the source of good voices. The more we learn to pray, the more we develop our spiritual senses which will help us to know the difference between good and bad voices.

Prayer is communication between God and us. Many people think it is only important to talk to God, but it is also important to wait and to be still before Him and to listen. Invite Jesus to speak to you by saying: "Lord Jesus, please speak to me. I am listening. Help me to understand your love and help me to love you."

Clear your mind and listen in silence. Let go of your scattered thoughts. It's not easy to clear your mind at first, but you will be able to do it if you keep practicing. Many times we do not receive answers because we do not ask and we cut God off after we ask, we hang up the phone and forget, to get an answer, we must listen.

Also, practice active listening through journaling. Prayer: "Lord Jesus speak to me. Help me to understand what you are trying to say." Then write down whatever comes to your mind. You can use your imagination while doing this and think what God may be speaking to you. Sometimes it may be Scriptures that come to your mind and whatever comes to your mind, if that seems to agree with the Bible, that's what God may be telling you. In addition, write down the questions you have for God. When you feel like you have an answer to a question, write it down. Again, that may be Scriptures. Then a month or so later, look back to see if you heard Him correctly or not.

Prayer: "Lord, Jesus, come into my heart. I open my heart to you. Teach me what is good and bad so I can learn to follow you, resist the bad voices and the devil's temptations. Teach me how to love you with all my heart, mind, soul and strength. Help me to follow your ways. Help me to have a peaceful life with your loving heart. I ask you to help me recognize how the Holy Spirit is leading my life to help others. I pray this in Jesus' name. Amen."

2. Bible reading

Hearing good voices is the result of good spiritual practice. Reading the Bible gives us good moral values and direction that we need to follow. When you hear the Scripture in your heart, God is speaking to you. You need to plant good thoughts by reading the Bible. Try reading one chapter a day from Proverbs for the next 30 days. In addition, start reading the Gospels: Matthew, Mark, Luke and John. Read the Bible for 30 minutes everyday and learn about Jesus for the next 30 days. This is to develop a habit of planting good thoughts in your mind so you will have less room to hear bad voices.

After 30 days, continue reading so you will develop a habit of listening to good voices from God. We need to learn what is right and wrong according to God's values which are much higher than human values. The Bible teaches us God's values. When we have God's values, we can avoid following bad voices and that's why it's important to read the Bible. If you don't understand the Bible, ask God for wisdom.

Prayer: "Lord Jesus, bless me with wisdom, knowledge, understanding, and revelation, so I can understand your Word and follow the path of love, peace and good life that will please you. Help me to help others who are hurting."

3. Develop a close relationship with Jesus

Developing a close relationship with the Lord helps us to recognize what He is trying to tell us. Jesus said, *"My sheep listen to my voice; I know them, and they follow me."* (John 10:27) Jesus seeks an intimate relationship with us and wants to speak to us; He wants to reveal His plans for our lives. People who do not hear or recognize God's voice are confused, causing lack of vision, feeling of emptiness inside and a misunderstanding of what God wants them to do with their lives. When we learn to listen and obey the plans that God reveals to us, we find purpose in life and fulfillment. Seeking Him with all our hearts is the key to listening: *"You will seek me and find me when you seek me with all your heart." (Jeremiah 29:13)*

In addition to reading the Gospels, read seven letters from Revelation chapters 2 and 3. Ask the Lord to reveal to you how He sees you. Prayer: "Lord Jesus, is there any words you have for me through this letter? Please help me to understand my spiritual condition. If there is anything that I need to change, please help me to understand and hear from you." Then in silence wait and listen. Don't give up even if you don't hear from Jesus immediately. Remember Solomon gave 1,000 offerings before God appeared to him in a dream and spoke to him. *(1 Kings 3:1-15)* You have to be persistent in prayer if you want to hear from God.

Tell Jesus you love Him throughout the day by saying, "Lord Jesus, I love you. Help me to love you and understand your love for me and for others." Have a notebook to write a love letter from Jesus. Write a love letter to Jesus. In this way, you will think about good thoughts. It will help you to understand Jesus' love so you can grow in love with Jesus.

If you don't have a relationship with Jesus you can invite Him into your heart and be saved. Prayer: "Lord Jesus, I am a sinner. Please forgive my sins. I give my heart to you. I surrender my life to you. Come into my heart and take control of my life. Fill me with the Holy Spirit and speak to me so I can obey you. I pray this in your name. Amen."

4. Think good and positive things about yourself and others

There are many bad voices that we need to resist. Let go of any critical and judgmental thoughts of yourself and others. Paul talked about how we should think: *"Finally, brothers, whatever is true, whatever is noble, whatever is right, whatever is pure, whatever is lovely, whatever is admirable--if anything is excellent or praiseworthy--think about such things." (Philippians 4:8)*

Start thinking good things about yourself and others. If you have bad attitudes towards yourself and others, you need to let go of those critical and judgmental thoughts. Change your thoughts from seeing negative things to positive things. Our culture can play a big role on how we think about ourselves and others. It's easy to develop a critical and negative attitude toward ourselves and others. But God values us and we should value ourselves and others.

What God created is good, but that doesn't mean we are all perfect. We need to learn to have positive attitudes and how to make positive choices so we can reflect God's image through us. To think positively, we need to understand Jesus' love. Ask the Lord to help you understand His love.

Prayer: "Lord Jesus, help me to see myself as you see me and help me to see others as you see them."

Our voice (self-talk) can be good or bad. Unless we are careful, we may be influenced by bad voices. We may be telling ourselves that we are unlovable and worthless. These voices will lead us to discontentment, turmoil and unhappiness. This is our sinful nature trying to see only bad things and devalue what God values. We have the capability to be bad and destroy our confidence if we are not careful. Treat yourself as God treats you. He treated you with the best gift of all – giving His only Son to die for you so you can be forgiven and have a peaceful relationship with Him.

Treat others as God would treat them – loving them and cherishing them. That's what Jesus did. He died on the cross for our sins because He loves us.

Prayer: "Lord Jesus, help me to love and respect myself and others, including those who have sinned against me. I forgive everyone who has hurt me. Please cleanse my heart so I can have a pure heart. Help me to know if there is any critical or negative attitude toward anyone including myself. Please help me to have love and compassion for everyone, including myself."

5. Practice silence and learn to quiet your mind

Practice silencing your thoughts and listening to God's good voice. *"Be still before the LORD and wait patiently for him." (Psalm 37:7a)*

To control your thoughts, you need to learn to shut off the voice channel and turn to the silence channel. This is difficult for many people. We are so used to noises and are not used to silence. But silence is what will help you develop an ear and heart to recognize good voices from bad voices. Practice silencing your thoughts 15 minutes a day and ask God to speak to you.

Prayer: "Lord Jesus, I am listening, please speak to me. Help me to recognize your voice and thoughts when you speak to me."

As you practice listening in silence, it will get easier as time goes by. You may not hear anything from the Lord for a while. If you wait long enough, you will recognize and hear His voice. This will give you understanding and help you to choose a good path. He will guide you to do good things to help others. He will guide you out of confusion bringing you out of darkness and into His light.

6. Control the voice you hear from outside

What we hear from the outside will affect what we hear in our minds. We can ask the Lord to help us.

Prayer: "Lord Jesus, please help me have the discernment and wisdom to choose what to listen to and what to avoid so I can hear good voices and have peace of mind instead of turmoil. Help me to understand your love to the fullest. Help me to have a great love for you and serve you without distraction."

The following are ways to control outside voices:

(1) Say good things: The person you will hear the most is yourself. Say good things and encouraging words to yourself and others. We can help others to hear good voices by saying encouraging words to them so they can hear good voices in their minds. Avoid any critical and judgmental words when you speak to others because what you say will affect others' minds positively or negatively (depending on what you say). What you say to others will affect your mind as well, so it's important that we say good things to others. Talk less and listen to others more. And instead of talking a lot, especially when you become critical of yourself or others, take time to listen.

(2) <u>Find positive people</u>: Try to spend more time with people who say good things about you and others. This is critical to your emotional health. Good voices are encouraging words from others. These voices help us to feel good about ourselves and it is good for our soul. If you are around people who have a positive outlook on life, the words you hear from them will become good voices in your mind.

(3) <u>Avoid negative people</u>: Avoid people who say critical and judgmental things about you. These people take away peace causing turmoil and pain. When you are around negative people, you will hear critical and judgmental words coming out of their mouths. Those bad words can stick in your mind and become a bad voice. Unfortunately, sometimes people with bad voices can be in our families. You also need to understand that they too, are the victims of hearing bad voices and are not aware of how to resist them. Learn from them; just don't be like them.

(4) <u>Watch, listen, and hear inspirational programs and media</u>: Watch TV or movies and listen to radio programs that will project good and educational things as much as possible. It's impossible not to listen to the news about what is happening, but we can control how much we hear. Read good books like the Bible, and other inspirational and educational books that help you develop high moral values. Avoid books that do not promote good moral values causing your mind to think about immoral thoughts. Anything that you think God would not approve of you reading, don't read it. We need to choose to listen to good voices and avoid hearing or seeing bad messages

including violence, sex and bad language on TV.

(5) <u>Attend church</u>: Learning about God is listening to good voices. Anything that shows us and reminds us of God's goodness and His grace are what we need to hear. Attend church worship services, Bible studies and prayer meetings to learn more about God so you can hear good voices.

7. Meditation

Find a Bible verse that helps you and encourages you. Write it out and put it on the wall or carry it in your purse or wallet to memorize it. The more you repeat the verse, the better you will be at hearing good voices and you will be encouraged and comforted. Ask the Lord what you need to meditate on. Before you read the Bible ask the Lord to give you the Bible verse.

Prayer: "Lord Jesus, help me to find a Bible verse that will help me hear your comforting voice."

Then read the Bible to find a short verse in which you can meditate day and night. When you feel you know the verse well, ask the Lord for another one to meditate on and memorize this verse as well. God speaks to us through the living Word, the Bible. He wants to build us up and wants to have a close relationship with us.

8. Process your painful thoughts

Our mind is like a room and has many file cabinets — one has good memories and the other one has bad and painful memories. The more we focus on our painful memories, the more we will hear bad voices. We need to take care of the painful memories one by one. We

DEVELOPING GOOD VOICES   / 39

need to forgive those who have hurt us. Thus, we don't clutter our thoughts or become overwhelmed by bad voices. This will help us to have more positive thoughts and enable us to let go of bad thoughts.

Prayer: "Lord Jesus, I need your help in letting go of my painful memories. I forgive everyone and I let go of my expectations of them. I need your forgiveness for holding resentment and anger. If there is anything I have done wrong, please help me to repent so I can be forgiven."

9. Forgive everyone, including yourself

Many people suffer from bad voices or accusing voices because they cannot forgive. You have to make the decision to forgive everyone. Jesus gave us direction on what to do when we get hurt. Forgive, pray and bless others. That doesn't mean you need to stay in an abusive relationship or a negative situation. Ask others to help you, but if they cannot help you, you need to remove yourself with the help of police or social services.

This forgiveness is for past experiences and we need to be careful not to justify our sin or the sinful actions of others. As you practice forgiveness, you will learn to hear good voices more than bad voices.

Prayer: "Lord Jesus, I made a decision to forgive everyone including myself. I ask you to bless me with your loving heart. Help me to see my spiritual condition so I can learn to be humble before you and to have compassion for myself and others. Reveal to me if there is any sin that I need to repent of. Please cleanse me and forgive me so there will be no distractions in our relationship."

10. Pay attention to the Holy Spirit's voice and obey Him

God gives us the Holy Spirit when we accept Jesus as our Lord and Savior. The Holy Spirit will guide and direct us to a good path. If you hear a voice or a thought asking you to do something, if it is a good thing and will help you and others grow in faith, it is coming from the Holy Spirit. It's more like some thoughts stay in the back of your mind that you know it's a good thing if you do it, but many times you may come up with excuses and put it off. If you ignore this good voice, it will keep coming back to you until you listen and when you obey it, you will have peace of mind. The Holy Spirit will tell us to do good things like to read the Bible, pray, forgive and do good things for others.

The Holy Spirit is a divine God and He lives within us. He can bless us with many spiritual insights through good voices. If you have not experienced the Holy Spirit, start writing a confession letter or take the time to ask God for forgiveness of your sins one by one. Go back to your childhood and ask the Lord to help you cleanse your heart and life.

Prayer: "Lord Jesus, please help me to repent. If there is any sin that I have not repented of, please show me so I can repent and make changes in my attitudes and behaviors. Cleanse my heart so I can be blessed with the Holy Spirit. Teach me what is right and wrong according to your values."

"Peter replied, 'Repent and be baptized, every one of you, in the name of Jesus Christ for the forgiveness of your sins. And you will receive the gift of the Holy Spirit.'" (Acts 2:38)

Developing a close relationship with the Holy Spirit is very important in hearing good voices.

11. Write a spiritual journal and ask for dream interpretation

To focus on listening to the good voice, we need to be active in listening to God's voice. Have a notebook and journal for your walk with the Lord. Write down prayers and what He is telling you. Also, write down your dreams and ask the Lord for interpretation.

Prayer: "Lord Jesus, please help me to understand why I had this dream. Is there anything you would like to say to me?" After prayer, quiet your mind and listen. Then write what He may be telling you. This spiritual practice can help you learn to hear the voice of God. Go back and read your dream journal later and see if you have heard from the Lord or not. Even if you don't hear anything, keep asking the same question, then God will give you understanding.

The Holy Spirit gives us dreams to direct us and to help us understand our spiritual condition; they can also reveal something concerning our future or the future of our loved ones, so we will know what to pray and be prepared to handle difficulties or joy in life.

For those who suffer from nightmares, read the Bible and pray more. The devil torments people by giving them nightmarish dreams, but prayer is a powerful weapon against him. However, not all nightmares are from the devil, God can also show us what is happening in our spiritual world, so we can pray and grow.

12. Serve others

People who do not have a clear purpose can be bored and suffer from bad voices. Learn to use your time wisely and learn how to control your thoughts. Helping others who are in need of your care helps you to develop positive attitudes and good thoughts. God has plans for each one of us and He wants us to love Him and love our neighbors. If we follow His loving plans to help others who are hurting, we will be giving less room for bad thoughts and voices.

God has plans for you. He says, "'For I know the plans I have for you,' declares the Lord, 'Plans to prosper you and not to harm you, plans to give you hope and a future. Then you will call upon me and come and pray to me, and I will listen to you. You will seek me and find me when you seek me with all your heart. I will be found by you,' declares the Lord.'" (Jeremiah 29:11-14a)

"Then Jesus came to them and said, 'All authority in heaven and on earth has been given to me. Therefore go and make disciples of all nations, baptizing them in the name of the Father and of the Son and of the Holy Spirit, and teaching them to obey everything I have commanded you. And surely I am with you always, to the very end of the age.'" (Matthew 28:18-20)

God gave you the gift of life so you can use it to help others. Volunteer to help others in the community, church or in a mission. Jesus gave us clear directions on how to live a good life. We are to help the poor, sick, prisoners and others who are in need of Christ.

Jesus said, "'I needed clothes and you clothed me, I was sick and you looked after me, I was in prison and you came to visit me.' Then the righteous will answer him, 'Lord, when did we see you hungry and feed you, or thirsty and give you something to drink? When did we see you a stranger and invite you in, or needing clothes and clothe you? When did we see you sick or in prison and go to visit you?' The King will reply, 'I tell you the truth, whatever you did for one of the least of these *brothers of mine, you did for me.'" (Matthew 25:36-40)*

Prayer: "Lord Jesus, I surrender my life and everything to you. Open my heart, so I can listen to your voice and understand your plans for me. What do you want me to do with my life? How can I love you and serve you? Please give me a clear direction and open the doors for me so I can serve you. Surround me with good people so they can help me and mentor me spiritually. I surrender all my plans because you have better plans for me. Help me to have your visions and dreams and to help many who are hurting. Help me to bring many people to Christ. Help me to accomplish your will. I pray this in Jesus' name. Amen."

Chapter 6

How God Speaks to Our Senses

Where do these good voices come from? I believe they come from God who made us. He is guiding us to do good and live a happy life by making good choices and following His ways, not our own. Everyone hears good voices. They hear because God wants to speak to everyone. God speaks to our spiritual senses. When God created us, He made us with a built-in communication like an antenna so He can speak to us. Spiritual senses work closely with our mind where we hear different voices; thoughts, intellect, emotions, feelings, desires and conscience.

Can we develop spiritual senses?

Paul prays so others can be enlightened. I believe enlightenment has something to do with understanding what we receive through our spiritual senses. Here is Paul's prayer: *"I pray also that the eyes of your heart may be enlightened in order that you may know the hope to which he has called you, the riches of his glorious inheritance in the saints."* (*Ephesians 1:18*)

The eyes of our heart are our spiritual senses and God can help us open them by giving us wisdom to understand what He wants us to do. Why would anyone believe that there is a God and accept that Jesus died for their sins? That sounds illogical except for those whose "eyes of the heart" are opened, have faith in God, and have accepted the spiritual truth from the Bible.

Our understanding works closely with our

intellect. We use our reasoning ability to understand what we perceive as right or wrong. We feel bad when we do wrong and that means our conscience is telling us we made a mistake. Everyone's conscience has different degrees of what is right and wrong. Our conscience can be enlightened by the knowledge of the Scripture and through the Holy Spirit's guidance.

The Holy Spirit helps us open our spiritual senses to understand what God's values are. We can learn and accept things that we cannot explain with human wisdom. That acceptance is the Holy Spirit working with our spiritual senses. When the Holy Spirit opens our hearts, we can understand the things that we were unable to understand before.

Our spiritual senses closely works with the Holy Spirit. Paul talks about how the Holy Spirit reveals things to us. He wrote, "*However, as it is written: 'No eye has seen, no ear has heard, no mind has conceived what God has prepared for those who love him' – but God has revealed it to us by his Spirit. The Spirit searches all things, even the deep things of God. For who among men knows the thoughts of a man except the man's spirit within him? In the same way no one knows the thoughts of God except the Spirit of God. We have not received the spirit of the world but the Spirit who is from God, that we may understand what God has freely given us. This is what we speak, not in words taught us by human wisdom but in words taught by the Spirit, expressing spiritual truths in spiritual words. The man without the Spirit does not accept the things that come from the Spirit of God, for they are foolishness to him, and he cannot understand them, because they are spiritually discerned. The spiritual man makes judgments about all things, but he himself is not subject to any man's judgment: 'For who has known the mind of the Lord that he may instruct him?' But we have the mind of Christ."* (1 Corinthians 2:9-16)

Paul boldly said that he has the mind of Christ. This is possible when the Holy Spirit reveals God's heart. Even though everyone has built-in spiritual senses, not everyone has developed them or can recognize them. There are different degrees of spiritual senses which depends on the persons' knowledge of the Word of God, and their relationship with the Lord, how they pay attention to the Holy Spirit's leading in their life, and how much time is spent in prayer and reflection.

God speaks to our spiritual senses through good voices, thoughts and feelings as well

We are made in the image of God. The spiritual senses we have are a part of God's image in us. He blessed us with spiritual senses so we can communicate with the Lord. Spiritual senses will help us understand what God is trying to tell us. He is sending signals that He is talking to us through spiritual senses so we can learn to listen. Whether you will be able to hear the small voice of God through your spiritual senses or not depends on how much you pay attention to your built-in spiritual senses.

We have to choose whether or not we will pay attention to our feelings and emotions that are filling our minds and hearts with different messages. We can accept God's signals by asking for His strength to obey, or we can ignore and reject them to follow our own desires and feelings.

The following are some ways in which God speaks to our spiritual senses. The more you pay attention to the signal in your spiritual sense, the more you will be able to understand what God is trying to tell you.

1. Restless feelings

When you feel restless, God is trying to get your attention. He has some message for you to listen to. You need to spend time asking the Lord what He is trying to tell you.

Many times God got my attention through restless feelings. As soon as I have this restless feeling, I immediately stop talking to God and try to listen and ask the Lord, "What is it Lord that you want to tell me?" I spend time in silence and try to listen to Him until I hear from the Lord. Usually, He has something to say to me. Sometimes He gave me assignments or helped me make changes in my attitudes and behaviors. I have learned to value the time of waiting and listening.

2. Feeling something is missing in your life

When you feel you are missing something, God is trying to tell you that you need to make some changes in your life. Examine the following areas: (1) Do you have a close relationship with Jesus? (2) Are you using your gifts to serve the Lord to the fullest? (3) Are you trying to develop a godly character and have a peaceful relationship with others?

First, you may be missing a relationship with the Lord. If you don't have a relationship with Jesus, you can invite him.

Prayer: "Lord Jesus, I give my life to you. Please come into my heart. Forgive me for all my sins and fill me with the Holy Spirit. Please help me to know what you want me to do with my life. Help me to love you and serve you."

If you have accepted Jesus as your Lord and you still feel you are missing something, you may not have a close relationship with Jesus. Get to know Jesus by reading the Bible, especially the four Gospels (Matthew, Mark, Luke and John) and ask the Holy Spirit to give you wisdom to understand it.

Prayer: "Holy Spirit, help me to know Jesus. Help me to understand the Bible. Help me to love Jesus and serve Him."

Second, if you have a close relationship with the Lord, and you still feel something is missing, you may not be using your gifts to the fullest. If you focus only on yourself and your family, you are not fully using your gifts. Find out how you can help others.

Prayer: "Holy Spirit, teach me what I need to do to serve Jesus. Open the doors for me."

Third, see how you are spending your time and see if there is anything that you need to change in your attitudes or words that you use and how you relate to others. Paul gives us directions on how we should live and you can reflect and see which area God is telling you to make changes in your life.

"The acts of the sinful nature are obvious: sexual immorality, impurity and debauchery; idolatry and witchcraft; hatred, discord, jealousy, fits of rage, selfish ambition, dissensions, factions and envy; drunkenness, orgies, and the like. I warn you, as I did before, that those who live like this will not inherit the kingdom of God. But the fruit of the Spirit is love, joy, peace, patience, kindness, goodness, faithfulness, gentleness and self-control. Against such things there is no

law. Those who belong to Christ Jesus have crucified the sinful nature with its passions and desires. Since we live by the Spirit, let us keep in step with the Spirit. Let us not become conceited, provoking and envying each other." (Galatians 5:19-26)

You cannot have a close relationship with the Lord if you are being critical and judgmental of yourself and others. You need to make changes in your attitudes and behaviors.

Prayer: "Lord Jesus, please give me wisdom to know what is missing in my life. Teach me so I will know which area I need to make changes in and help me to make those changes. Help me to have a loving attitude toward myself and others."

3. Feeling that God is not listening to your prayers

When you feel that God is not listening to your prayers, there is something you need to take care of before you present your request to Him. Stop requesting what you have been asking for. Ask Him to speak to you and reveal what He wants you to hear. Wait in silence until He speaks to you. You don't always have to hold still when you are waiting. You can walk around and clear your mind and wait in silence.

The fact that you feel and understand that God is not listening to your prayer shows that you are getting the message from the Lord and you need to understand His heart. Maybe you have sin in your life or attitudes you need to repent. Or you may need to forgive or let go of something that you are holding on to.

Prayer: "Lord Jesus, I pray that you give me understanding. Why do I feel you are not listening to my prayer? Is there anything that I need to take care of?

Please speak to me."

Start reading the Bible and ask the Lord to give you wisdom to understand what He is trying to tell you through the Bible.

4. Feeling of anxiousness

God is telling you to turn to Jesus to find peace. There are times people suffer from anxiousness because they have faced a life crisis. It's normal to have these feelings when you are in crisis but God already has answers for all our problems and He is telling us that we can turn to Him for healing.

Jesus said, *"Come to me, all you who are weary and burdened, and I will give you rest. Take my yoke upon you and learn from me, for I am gentle and humble in heart, and you will find rest for your souls. For my yoke is easy and my burden is light." (Matthew 11:28-30)*

If everything is going well with you but you still don't have peace, there is something God is trying to tell you. You need to turn to God, listen and He will tell you what to do to find peace. Sometimes He may be signaling that you are emotionally and spiritually depleted and need to spend time with Him.

5. Feeling sad and lacking joy

God is telling you that you lack something and you need to do something about it. True joy comes from loving the Lord, loving ourselves and serving others. There could be many reasons that you feel depressed or lack joy. Consider the following and see which category you fit in:

(1) Lack of reading the Word of God: You are not reading

the Word of God to feed your spiritual hunger. God said when you seek Him earnestly, you will find Him. When you find Him, you will be filled with joy. Paul said rejoice in the Lord and if you haven't found joy in the Lord, it's time to read the Bible to learn about Jesus.

(2) Lack of prayer: You may not be spending enough time with the Lord in prayer to find joy. Take the time to wait in silence and ask Him to speak to you. When He speaks to you, you will find joy.

(3) Not using your gifts to serve: You may not be using your gifts to serve the Lord. The joy of serving is missing in many people who do not use their gifts to the fullest. When you are using your gifts the way God wants you to, you will be filled with joy.

(4) You may be grieving: You may be hurting emotionally from the loss of something or someone. While grieving there is a need to repair your broken heart. You will have many emotions when you deal with grief and loss. You will need to take care of all the emotions that are related to grief. Also, you need to let go of your loved ones and place everything in God's hands in order for you to be healed; then you will find peace and joy.

(5) You may need to forgive: You may be angry or resentful about some situation and unable to forgive or unwilling to forgive. Until you forgive, anger will control your heart and life. Anger doesn't bring joy, it brings sadness and depressive thoughts and takes away our peace.

(6) Your priorities are out of order: You may rely on something or someone for joy and fulfillment. People

and things have limitations on how much joy they bring. This type of joy is temporary. You need to rely on the Lord for complete joy.

(7) <u>You need to be filled with the Holy Spirit</u>: The Holy Spirit can bless us with spiritual joy when we love and serve the Lord. I am talking about spiritual joy. When you are walking with God and obeying the Lord, from time to time the Holy Spirit will help you experience this joy. It is an overflowing joy. When I work on the book projects the Holy Spirit asks me to work on, I feel the joy that no one can give but God. At times, I am so filled with joy that I have to say, "Calm me down Lord. Calm me down. I am just too excited because you bless me so much." I know this joy I feel is confirmation from the Holy Spirit that I am on the right path.

6. Feeling depressed

If you are depressed, God is telling you that there is something that you may need to do, but you are not doing it. Seek God's wisdom by reading the Bible and talk to pastors or chaplains or a professional counselor who can help you sort out your problems.

There may be many reasons why people get depressed. As you read through some of the reasons listed here, ask God to tell you what changes you need to make.

(1) <u>You may have medical problems</u>: Maybe you have chemical or neurological problems or the medicine you are taking is affecting your moods. Find out from your doctor what you should do to correct your

problem.

(2) <u>You may be living in sin</u>: When you live in sin, you are not going to have happy feelings or have peace in your heart. Stop using alcohol or drugs to numb your pain. Any addictive lifestyles which promote ungodly behaviors is sin. If you feel bad about what you are doing, the Holy Spirit is convicting you that you are not living a godly life. Prayer: "Lord Jesus, if there is any sin I need to repent of, please help me to repent and make changes so I can find peace. Help me to live a life that is free of addiction and any ungodly lifestyle habits." If you don't suffer from addiction, but sad feelings persist, you may need to ask the Lord if you are not obeying Him in any way. You have to forgive everyone including yourself to find peace. Let go of your resentments, anger, bitterness, and hate so you can be free from a prison of sadness.

(3) <u>You may suffer from twisted thinking which is a bad voice</u>: You may have accepted the twisted voice of the devil. Many depressed people suffer from negative and critical thoughts because they have not learned to recognize the devil's destructive voice. You may have accepted and believed the bad voices. These bad voices tell people that their life is not worthwhile and that their problems are impossible for them to solve. These bad voices even twist the Word of God so that some people have a difficult time reading the Bible. Reject any voices that hinder you from reading the Bible. You need to change your helpless and hopeless thoughts to God's positive thoughts. Go to God and ask for help and keep reading the Bible. Also, you need healing from whatever is hurting you. It could be

changing your thought patterns by proclaiming God's victory over your life. Memorize what Paul wrote and make it your thoughts: *"I can do everything through him who gives me strength."* *(Philippians 4:13)* Prayer: "Lord Jesus, help me to see the big picture so I will not be disappointed, discouraged or depressed. Help me to find hope, comfort, healing and encouragement in you so I can have spiritual freedom in Christ. Help me to see the positive in all things because you are with me and you are always on my side. "

(4) <u>You may suffer from spiritual oppression</u>: God is telling you that you need to take authority. Jesus has given us power and authority to be free from spiritual oppression. There are people who suffer from depression for no apparent reason whatsoever. Sometimes that is the indication of spiritual oppression. Resist the devil in Jesus' name, start reading the Bible, pray and proclaim victory in Christ. God will give you spiritual strength to find freedom and peace.

(5) <u>You may be holding onto grief and the loss of something or someone</u>: God is telling you that you need to rely on the Lord for healing and strength and to let go of your loved ones. You need to give to God everything and everyone you care about including your loved ones who have passed. You can pray that God will take away all the desires and the pain related to the person you love. Prayer: "Lord Jesus, I am hurting and I need your help. I give my loved one to you. Please take away all my desire and wanting to be with my loved one. Heal my broken heart and help me to focus on you and the blessings you have given

me instead of looking into what I have lost. Please take away all my pain and I ask that you heal my wounds. Help me to give you everything that is hindering my love for you. I thank you for healing my mind and heart."

(6) An abusive situation: You may be living in an abusive situation or working in an abusive environment. You need God's wisdom to make the appropriate changes to stop the abuse. You might have to ask others to help you if you cannot do it yourself. You might have to find another job if that is the cause of your depression.

There are many reasons for depressed feelings. One thing is clear, you have received the message from the Lord that you need to make some changes in either your thoughts or in your lifestyle. God has the power to help you, but there are some changes you need to make for you to experience healing.

7. Feeling you are neglecting to do something

The Holy Spirit is trying to tell you that you are ignoring Him on some issue. Maybe He told you to do something and you came up with excuses and have not done it. Spend time reading the Bible. Ask the Lord what He wants you to do. If you know what He asked you to do, it's best to obey Him so you can find peace. He will keep speaking to you until you obey Him. The Holy Spirit always has better ideas than ours, and it's good that we can learn to be humble and be obedient.

8. Feeling confused

God is telling you that it's time to read the Word of God and listen to Him to find out why you are confused. Spiritual attacks can also make you feel confused. You need to pray to the Lord for healing so you can have a clear mind. Many confused people seek advice from others. What they need is to turn to God and read the Word of God and resist confusing voices. You need to develop a close relationship with the Holy Spirit.

Prayer: "Holy Spirit, please help me to have clear thinking. Surround me with angels and protect me from all confusion and fear. Show me if there is any area I need to change. Help me to have a clear understanding of what is happening."

When you make decisions in life, remember that human wisdom has limitations, but God's wisdom can tell you what you need to do to find the answers. Spend more time praying and asking God specific questions every day until you get the answers. Your persistent prayers pay off and you will see the results. Ask for God's wisdom and direction. Make plans after that and see if you feel resistance in your heart when you try to carry them out.

If something you plan to do doesn't give you peace after you've prayed, wait and listen to the Lord and ask for direction. Keep praying until you hear from the Lord.

"Trust in the LORD with all your heart and lean not on your own understanding; in all your ways acknowledge him, and he will make your paths straight." (Proverbs 3:5-6)

9. Feeling you can't love yourself

God is telling you that you need to see yourself as

God sees you. You may have been hurt by others or influenced by the bad voices and bad spirits that tell you that you are no good and you don't deserve love. Whatever the reason, you need to read the Bible more to understand God's love.

Jesus said, *"For God so loved the world that he gave his one and only Son, that whoever believes in him shall not perish but have eternal life." (John 3:16)*

John also tells us about how much God loves us. *"This is love: not that we loved God, but that he loved us and sent his Son as an atoning sacrifice for our sins. 'Dear friends, since God so loved us, we also ought to love one another. No one has ever seen God; but if we love one another, God lives in us and his love is made complete in us. We know that we live in him and he in us, because he has given us of his Spirit." (1 John 4:10-13)*

You need to learn to see yourself as God sees you, as a beloved and precious child of God. He loves you to the point that He sent His son to pay for your sins so you can have a peaceful relationship with Him. Learn to love and respect yourself as a child of God. Rebuke the spirit of hatred in the name of Jesus and tell it to leave. Find the Scriptures that tells about God's love and start to memorize them. Ask the Holy Spirit to teach you how to love yourself.

10. Feeling overwhelmed

God is telling you that you need to take care of things so that problems don't pile up in your heart. Ask the Lord to show you the things that are bothering you. Take care of your issues one by one so you don't feel overwhelmed.

Prayer: "Lord Jesus, I give everything to you. Please help me to know what I need to work on to find peace."

11. Feeling stuck, addicted and obsessed

When people feel stuck, helpless and hopeless, God is telling them to turn to Him for healing and to change their lifestyle. If you are suffering from alcohol, drugs, violence or abuse, feeling stuck is one of the feelings that you will suffer from.

Write a confession letter to God and ask Him to forgive you for each sin you have committed and ask Him to cleanse you.

Prayer: "Lord Jesus, please help me to know if there is any sin that I need to repent of. Forgive me for all the years I have ignored you. Forgive me for my addictive, ungodly, sinful lifestyle. Help me to choose you to find healing and comfort that I need, instead of numbing my pain with destructive things. Please take away the desire to rely on alcohol or drugs or even people. Help me so I can repair my relationship with you and with others."

People who suffer from addiction, or love something or someone more than God, desperately need to turn and love God more than anyone or anything. When you use drugs and violence to numb your pain or to make yourself feel better, you are telling God that you are not relying on Him.

The Scripture tells us how to live. *"Make every effort to live in peace with all men and to be holy; without holiness no one will see the Lord. See to it that no one misses the grace of God and that no bitter root grows up to cause trouble and defile many." (Hebrews 12:14-15)*

For those who feel they cannot be freed of an addictive lifestyle, they must rely on the Lord for healing. You have to make a decision to follow the Lord instead of your own desires. *"'If you can?' said Jesus. 'Everything is possible for him who believes.'"* (Mark 9:23) You can be free from any addiction with God's help. It's a process. For some people, it might take time to clean up but some can quit immediately. It's up to you to make that decision. God cannot stop you if you continuously go back to your old lifestyle. You have to follow God's voice (asking you to live a holy life) and use your gift of life for giving glory to God instead of wasting it away. Many people who suffer from addiction are freed by making the decision to obey the Lord. He will help you if you are willing to make changes.

12. Feeling of discontentment

God is telling you that there is something that you are neglecting or that you need to make changes in some areas. You should pray and ask God to show you what changes He wants you to make. It may be that you need to make a change in your job. It may be that you need to change your attitudes, words and lifestyle according to God's values.

When you start making changes, the Holy Spirit will start filling your heart with happiness and contentment. What is important is obedience to the Lord. A deep sense of happiness and contentment is the result of loving God and serving Him to the fullest. Paul said he learned to be content in every situation. *"I know what it is to be in need, and I know what it is to have plenty. I have learned the secret of being content in any and every situation, whether well fed or hungry, whether living in plenty or in want." (Philippians 4:12)*

We can learn from Paul and learn how to be content by relying on the Lord to provide everything.

Prayer: "Lord Jesus, please help me to know if there is anything I need to change. Help me to have the wisdom and courage to follow your lead in my life."

13. Feeling a lack of confidence

God may be telling you that you are depending on your own wisdom and strength instead of relying on Him. Paul was encouraging others with the confidence that God was going to do all that He told him.

He said, *"So keep up your courage, men, for I have faith in God that it will happen just as he told me." (Acts 27:25)* He knew God was speaking to him because he had a close relationship with Him. Paul followed his calling to spread the gospel and Jesus started speaking to him to keep up the courage. Our confidence comes from the Lord. God encouraged Joshua after Moses died.

"No one will be able to stand up against you all the days of your life. As I was with Moses, so I will be with you; I will never leave you nor forsake you. Be strong and courageous, because you will lead these people to inherit the land I swore to their forefathers to give them. Be strong and very courageous. Be careful to obey all the law my servant Moses gave you; do not turn from it to the right or to the left, that you may be successful wherever you go. Do not let this Book of the Law depart from your mouth; meditate on it day and night, so that you may be careful to do everything written in it. Then you will be prosperous and successful. Have I not commanded you? Be strong and courageous. Do not be terrified; do not be

discouraged, for the LORD your God will be with you wherever you go." (Joshua 1:5-9)

Read this Scripture whenever you feel you need God's encouragement and be obedient to the Lord.

14. Feeling that your prayers are not going to be answered

God may be telling you that you are not going to get what you are asking for. Or you may be doubting. Or you may not have heard God's clear voice on this matter.

Read the Bible to see if what you are asking is for your own sinful or selfish reasons. If it is, don't expect that God will answer your prayers. You need to change the prayers so that God's will is part of your life. If what you are asking is a good thing, even though the circumstances seem to be impossible, God can change it. You need to ask the Lord to show you the big picture so that you will find peace about the situation.

Also, He will not always answer our prayers the way we ask because He has better plans for us. Wait and listen in silence until you can get the answers from the Lord. You don't always have to sit still to be in silence. You can walk around and do other things while you quiet your mind and listen.

15. Feeling that you lack desire and passion to serve God

God is telling you that you have a lack of love and passion for the lost. We need to pray that we will have God's heart so we have the desire and passion to reach out to the lost. He can give you that desire as you decide to follow Jesus.

When I suffered from lukewarm faith, I had no desire or passion for the lost, but deep in my mind, I knew what I wanted to see. I have had a burning desire to see a revival since I came to America. God explained to me later that He was the one who planted the seed in my heart to see a revival. What I wanted to see is what He wanted to see in me. He did start a revival in my heart and gave me the desire to lead many people to the Lord.

16. Feeling stuck in the pain of grief and loss

God is telling you that you need healing from your broken heart. Grieving is natural when you lose your loved ones. You need to process all of the emotions that are related to grief, like anger, resentment, bitterness, blame, regrets, forgiveness, attachment, letting go, etc. Take care of all emotions that are related to grief with God's help, so you can experience healing. If you are continuously immobilized, you need to take care of your hurts and pain with His help. God can heal your broken heart so you can function normally and live a life filled with joy and peace again. He has done that for me.

17. Feeling a desperate need from others' encouragement from others

At times we need encouragement from others and it's important to have positive people give us feedback. But if you are desperately looking for encouragement and affirmation all the time and your happiness relies on other people, you need to work on your relationship with God. God is telling you that what you really need is not other people's encouragement but His encouraging words. Why? Eventually, people are limited on how much they can give. God is the one who can give us what we really need. You need to seek His love and encouragement through the Word of God.

As you get to know the Lord through the Scriptures and develop a close relationship with Jesus through prayer, He will comfort and encourage you. Jesus encouraged Paul through a vision. *"One night the Lord spoke to Paul in a vision: 'Do not be afraid; keep on speaking, do not be silent. For I am with you, and no one is going to attack and harm you, because I have many people in this city.' So Paul stayed for a year and a half, teaching them the word of God." (Acts 18:9-11)*

God will encourage you through others when you need it if you are walking with the Lord. But you will be disappointed if you are only seeking the encouragement of others. We all have the desire to be loved and encouraged but the Lord is saying that we need to rely on Him, not people. So, turn to the Lord and learn to listen to Him. He will fill all your needs; you can let go of your desire for the approval of others. Jesus is all you need to find happiness and fulfillment. So, knowing what to do when you feel lonely or feel discouraged because other people didn't give you what you wanted to have, rely on the Lord to fill you.

18. Feeling a lack of direction

God is telling you that it's time to listen to Him for direction and learn what you are called to do. Get to know Jesus. He is the one who will help you to know what you are supposed to do. Read the Bible, it will give you a clear direction. We need to love God and love our neighbors. Jesus gave us clear direction. Loving God has to be your first priority in life. Ask the Holy Spirit to help you to understand your calling. Find out what you are good at and what gifts you have. Your calling depends on your gifts. Don't just wait. Find out how you can serve others and as you serve, your calling will come clear to you.

19. Feel you are being disciplined

God is trying to get your attention by allowing you to feel that He is disciplining you. If you recognize it and learn to listen and obey, you will be blessed. If you ignore the warning, you will suffer the consequences.

"And you have forgotten that word of encouragement that addresses you as sons: 'My son, do not make light of the Lord's discipline, and do not lose heart when he rebukes you, because the Lord disciplines those he loves, and he punishes everyone he accepts as a son.' Endure hardship as discipline; God is treating you as sons. For what son is not disciplined by his father? If you are not disciplined (and everyone undergoes discipline), then you are illegitimate children and not true sons. Moreover, we have all had human fathers who disciplined us and we respected them for it. How much more should we submit to the Father of our spirits and live! " (Hebrews 12:5-9)

20. Feeling a lack of spiritual understanding

God is telling you to rely on Him for spiritual wisdom. He can speak to us when we reflect or meditate on the Word of God. The Holy Spirit will help you understand what you didn't before. However, we need to watch out because not all of the voices we hear are the voices of God. Sometimes the devil can twist the Word of God as he did when he was tempting Jesus. We need to ask God for discernment.

Prayer: "Lord Jesus, help me to have the gift of

discernment so I will understand what is right and wrong according to your values and please help me to hear the voice of the Holy Spirit."

21. Your conscience is bothering you

When you fall into sin, you feel guilt and shame. God is telling you that you have done something wrong and need to repent and change your ways. After you have repented, been forgiven by God, and are not living in the same sin any more, you should not be feeling guilt or shame. The Holy Spirit convicts our sins and that's what we need to hear from Him.

Remember, the devil likes to accuse you of your past sin to torment you. Reject the voices that tell you that God will not forgive you. You just need to rely on God for forgiveness and reject any condemning voices. *"If we confess our sins, he is faithful and just and will forgive us our sins and purify us from all unrighteousness." (1 John 1:9)*

22. You have joy from the Lord

When you are walking with the Lord and do what He wants you to do, sometimes you will experience unspeakable joy. This is God speaking to you that you are on the right path. When the Holy Spirit speaks to us through spiritual senses, your sense of peace, joy, love, faith and contentment is not comparable to any of your regular senses or feelings. Peace, love and joy can be felt by your whole being. Some describe it as oceans of joy, blankets of love, or being wrapped in love. God is communicating with you that He is rejoicing with you and your obedience.

Chapter 7

God Has Many Languages

There are many other languages that God uses to speak to us. They are all good voices that give us direction to live a good life.

We have many unspoken languages through observing people's facial expressions, sign language, tone of voice and body gestures. God has many more languages. The more we recognize God's language, the more we can understand what He is trying to tell us.

God wants us to listen and hear Him. *"Come, all you who are thirsty, come to the waters; and you who have no money, come, buy and eat! Come, buy wine and milk without money and without cost. Why spend money on what is not bread, and your labor on what does not satisfy? Listen, listen to me, and eat what is good, and your soul will delight in the richest of fare. Give ear and come to me; hear me, that your soul may live. I will make an everlasting covenant with you, my faithful love promised to David."* (Isaiah 55:1–3)

The languages God uses to speak to us

1. The Bible

God speaks to us through the words from the Bible. The Bible talks about who God is, what He does and what He expects of us. It's very important to read the Bible, because it will give you spiritual wisdom, knowledge, understanding, revelation and spiritual strength. It is essential to know God. Unless you know Him, how can you guess what He will say?

Read the Bible to learn how God speaks to people in different ways. The Word of God transformed many people in the Bible. Daniel was repenting for his nation after he started reading the Bible. The angel explained the Bible and called the Word of the Bible, "The Book of Truth." *"But first I will tell you what is written in the Book of Truth." (Daniel 10:21a)*

"This is what the LORD says: 'Heaven is my throne, and the earth is my footstool. Where is the house you will build for me? Where will my resting place be? Has not my hand made all these things, and so they came into being?' declares the LORD. 'This is the one I esteem: he who is humble and contrite in spirit, and trembles at my word.'" (Isaiah 66:1-2)

The Holy Spirit will remind us of the Scriptures. They will guide us. When you are reminded of some Bible verses that give you comfort or direction, pay attention to them.

2. Dreams

God can speak to us through dreams. He uses this method of communication a lot, but many people ignore it. *"He said, 'Listen to my words: 'When a prophet of the LORD is among you, I reveal myself to him in visions, I speak to him in dreams.'" (Numbers 12:6)*

God can also give us interpretations of dreams. While in prison, Joseph interpreted the dreams of others and gave credit to God. He told others that the interpretation of dreams belongs to God. *(Genesis 40:1-23)*

Jacob had a dream and God spoke to him. *"Jacob left Beersheba and set out for Haran. When he reached a certain place, he stopped for the night because the sun had set. Taking one of the stones there, he put it under his head and lay down to sleep. He had a dream in which he saw a stairway resting on the earth, with its top reaching to heaven, and the angels of God were ascending and descending on it. There above it stood the LORD, and he said: 'I am the LORD, the God of your father Abraham and the God of Isaac. I will give you and your descendants the land on which you are lying. Your descendants will be like the dust of the earth, and you will spread out to the west and to the east, to the north and to the south. All peoples on earth will be blessed through you and your offspring. I am with you and will watch over you wherever you go, and I will bring you back to this land. I will not leave you until I have done what I have promised you.' When Jacob awoke from his sleep, he thought, 'Surely the LORD is in this place, and I was not aware of it.' He was afraid and said, 'How awesome is this place! This is none other than the house of God; this is the gate of heaven.' Early the next morning Jacob took the stone he had placed under his head and set it up as a pillar and poured oil on top of it. He called that place Bethel, though the city used to be called Luz. Then Jacob made a vow, saying, 'If God will be with me and will watch over me on this journey I am taking and will give me food to eat and clothes to wear so that I return safely to my father's house, then the LORD will be my God and this stone that I have set up as a pillar will be God's house, and of all that you give me I will give you a tenth.'" (Genesis 28:10-22)*

Jacob also had visions and dreams and understood what God was saying. God gave Jacob confirmation that going down to Egypt to see Joseph was what he was supposed to do, and that God was going with him.

Not all dreams are from the Lord but they are affected by our memories, thoughts, environment and lifestyles; also demons can torment people through nightmares. Prayer, seeking the Lord through Scriptures and relying on the Lord will bring healing from nightmares. If you feel you are living in sin, it's time to repent and turn to the Lord for healing. You cannot grow spiritually and have a close relationship with the Lord when you are living in sin. You are opening the door for the devil and sometimes our nightmares are telling us that we need to change. As you grow in your close relationship with the Lord, you will be strong and be freed from nightmares.

3. Visions

God can speak to us about His greatness through visions. Isaiah was praying in the sanctuary and saw the Lord. *"In the year that King Uzziah died, I saw the Lord seated on a throne, high and exalted, and the train of his robe filled the temple. Above him were seraphs, each with six wings: With two wings they covered their faces, with two they covered their feet, and with two they were flying. And they were calling to one another: 'Holy, holy, holy is the LORD Almighty; the whole earth is full of his glory.' At the sound of their voices the doorposts and thresholds shook and the temple was filled with smoke. 'Woe to me!' I cried. 'I am ruined! For I am a man of unclean lips, and I live among a people of unclean lips, and my eyes have seen the King, the LORD Almighty.'"* (Isaiah 6:1-5)

Having a vision is a gift from the Holy Spirit. *"In the last days, God says, I will pour out my Spirit on all people. Your sons and daughters will prophesy, your young men will see visions, your old men will dream dreams."* (Acts 2:17)

There are three kinds of visions: (1) We can see visions when our eyes are open. (2) We can have visions in our dreams. (3) We can have spiritual visions which is mental pictures and images that come to our mind with our eyes open or closed. All these visions that come from the Lord have messages. When we see visions, we need to ask the Lord for interpretations so we can understand what He is trying to tell us.

The devil also can give us visions, images and mental pictures that will lead us to sin, destruction and torment. Whenever you have destructive thoughts, hear voices, or see visions that are not from God, pray the Lord's Prayer again and again, especially the part: "Deliver us from evil."

4. Trance

This is between the awake and sleeping stage. Peter experienced this while he was praying. Peter had a vision while he was in a trance stage.

The Scripture says, *"About noon the following day as they were on their journey and approaching the city, Peter went up on the roof to pray. He became hungry and wanted something to eat, and while the meal was being prepared, he fell into a trance. He saw heaven opened and something like a large sheet being let down to earth by its four corners. It contained all kinds of four-footed animals, as well as reptiles of the earth and birds of the air. Then a voice told him, 'Get up, Peter. Kill and eat.' 'Surely not, Lord!' Peter replied. 'I have never eaten anything impure or unclean.' The voice spoke to him a second time, 'Do not call anything impure that God has made clean.' This happened three times, and immediately the sheet was taken back to heaven." (Acts 10:9-16)*

There is always a lesson when God speaks to us through a vision or mental pictures when our eyes are open or closed, wide awake, sleeping or even in a trance stage.

The lesson God wanted to teach Peter was to let go of his prejudice against gentiles. *"Then Peter began to speak: 'I now realize how true it is that God does not show favoritism but accepts men from every nation who fear him and do what is right." (Acts 10:34-35)*

5. Different languages

At the Pentecost, when the Holy Spirit came, the disciples of Jesus were filled with the Holy Spirit and they started speaking in different languages and proclaimed God's message. This gift was given so people could hear about Jesus in their own language. *(Acts 2:1-8)*

There is another kind of tongue that is not to proclaim God's message. It is a gift of language that helps a person to communicate with God. Paul wrote, *"For anyone who speaks in a tongue does not speak to men but to God. Indeed, no one understands him; he utters mysteries with his spirit." (1 Corinthians 14:2)*

6. Audible voices

When Moses saw the burning bush, he went closer to see what was happening. He then heard the voice of the Lord. God told Moses to take off his sandals because he was standing on holy ground. God spoke to Moses many times after that. God also spoke to Samuel. God can choose to speak to people in an audible voice.

"The LORD called Samuel a third time, and Samuel got up and went to Eli and said, 'Here I am; you called me.' Then Eli realized that the LORD was calling the boy. So Eli told Samuel, 'Go and lie down, and if he calls you, say, 'Speak, LORD, for your servant is listening.' So Samuel went and lay down in his place. The LORD came and stood there, calling as at the other times, 'Samuel! Samuel!' Then Samuel said, 'Speak, for your servant is listening.' And the LORD said to Samuel: 'See, I am about to do something in Israel that will make the ears of everyone who hears of it tingle.'" (1 Samuel

3:8-11)

7. Presence

God is always with us, but we feel His presence when He wants us to know that He is near. That's one way He speaks to us. When Solomon built the temple for the Lord, and people worshipped him, God's presence manifested as clouds.

"The trumpeters and singers joined in unison, as with one voice, to give praise and thanks to the LORD. Accompanied by trumpets, cymbals and other instruments, they raised their voices in praise to the LORD and sang: 'He is good; his love endures forever.' Then the temple of the LORD was filled with a cloud, and the priests could not perform their service because of the cloud, for the glory of the LORD filled the temple of God. Then Solomon said, 'The LORD has said that he would dwell in a dark cloud; I have built a magnificent temple for you, a place for you to dwell forever.'" (2 Chronicles 5:13-6:2)

8. Angels

God spoke to many people through angels. Cornelius' visit from an angel who told him to invite Peter to his house. *"At Caesarea there was a man named Cornelius, a centurion in what was known as the Italian Regiment. He and all his family were devout and God-fearing; he gave generously to those in need and prayed to God regularly. One day at about three in the afternoon he had a vision. He distinctly saw an angel of God, who came to him and said, 'Cornelius!' Cornelius stared at him in fear. 'What is it, Lord?' he asked. The angel answered, 'Your prayers and gifts to the poor have come up as a memorial offering before God. Now send men to Joppa to bring back a man named Simon who is called Peter. He is staying with Simon the tanner, whose house is by the sea.'" (Acts 10:1-6)*

When I saw an angel in my dream, it was the most beautiful being I have ever seen. All the beauty I had seen in people cannot be compared to the angel I saw. God gave me understanding that He sees people as beautiful in the same way as the angel.

9. The Holy Spirit's voice

God can speak to us in an audible voice. Most of the time we hear a small voice in our heart, it is the Holy Spirit speaking to us. It's like gentle whispers.

"The LORD said, 'Go out and stand on the mountain in the presence of the LORD, for the LORD is about to pass by.' Then a great and powerful wind tore the mountains apart and shattered the rocks before the LORD, but the LORD was not in the wind. After the wind there was an earthquake, but the LORD was not in the earthquake. After the earthquake came a fire, but the LORD was not in the fire. And after the fire came a gentle whisper. When Elijah heard it, he pulled his cloak over his face and went out and stood at the mouth of the cave. Then a voice said to him, 'What are you doing here, Elijah?'" (1 King 19:11-13)

Jesus teaches us that the Holy Spirit is our spiritual counselor, teacher, mentor, comforter, director and guide. Jesus can speak to us in our hearts but the Holy Spirit also speaks to us. Jesus said, *"If you love me, you will obey what I command. And I will ask the Father, and he will give you another Counselor to be with you forever--the Spirit of truth. The world cannot accept him, because it neither sees him nor knows him. But you know him, for he lives with you and will be in you." (John 14:15-17) "But the Counselor, the Holy Spirit, whom the Father will send in my name, will teach you all things and will remind you of everything I have said to you." (John 14:26)*

Not only does the Holy Spirit speak to us, He helps us to learn about Jesus. When we obey the Lord, we have a feeling of contentment, peace, joy and happiness which is a confirmation from the Holy Spirit that we are on the right path.

10. Knowledge

God speaks to our intellect by giving us knowledge to understand what we couldn't understand before. Paul talks about spiritual knowledge and instructs us how we can understand God's mind through the Holy Spirit. The reason Paul's letters touch us so much is He is speaking of spiritual knowledge. We understand what Paul is trying to say with the help from the Holy Spirit.

Paul wrote, *"Now to each one the manifestation of the Spirit is given for the common good. To one there is given through the Spirit the message of wisdom, to another the message of knowledge by means of the same Spirit." (1 Corinthians 12:7-8)*

How can a person gain spiritual knowledge? The Holy Spirit communicates to us about spiritual matters and we understand something we couldn't before.

11. Wisdom

God can give us spiritual wisdom to know spiritual matters. Understanding the Bible is an example. The Bible was a closed book for me for a long time. When God helped me to understand the Bible, it changed my life.

Paul talks about how the Holy Spirit can help us with spiritual wisdom. He wrote, *"We have not received the spirit of the world but the Spirit who is from God, that we may understand what God has freely given us. This is what we speak, not in words taught us by human wisdom but in words taught by the Spirit, expressing spiritual truths in spiritual words. The man without the Spirit does not accept the things that come from the Spirit of God, for they are foolishness to him, and he cannot understand them, because they are spiritually discerned." (1 Corinthians 2:12-14)*

One day I was leading a prayer meeting in a pod. We were sharing our prayer requests. The last woman who shared told me that she was wondering if God was real. She wanted some kind of sign that He was alive because she had a difficult time believing in God. We prayed that God would give her a sign. Within a week I was visiting the same housing unit. This woman who was asking God for a sign came up to me and said that God gave her a sign and He was real. She explained that she used to read the Bible and didn't understand what it was saying. Then after we prayed for her to receive the sign, suddenly the Bible stories came alive and it all made sense to her. I saw a big smile on her face. What she needed was the Holy Spirit's wisdom to understand what the Bible was saying.

12. Conviction

God is holy and He wants us to have a pure heart so He can bless us. The Holy Spirit reveals to us when we have fallen into sin and He grieves. Paul wrote, *"And do not grieve the Holy Spirit of God, with whom you were sealed for the day of redemption. Get rid of all bitterness, rage and anger, brawling and slander, along with every form of malice. Be kind and compassionate to one another, forgiving each other, just as in Christ God forgave you." (Ephesians 4:30-32)*

When we repent and ask God for forgiveness we are forgiven. *"If we confess our sins, he is faithful and just and will forgive us our sins and purify us from all unrighteousness." (1 John 1:9)*

13. Revelation

Revelation is something God reveals to people about what's going to happen or to give us understanding of spiritual reality or something that only God wants to share. The Bible is God's story of revelation to us. Paul prays for others to have revelation from the Lord. *"I keep asking that the God of our Lord Jesus Christ, the glorious Father, may give you the Spirit of wisdom and revelation, so that you may know him better. I pray also that the eyes of your heart may be enlightened in order that you may know the hope to which he has called you, the riches of his glorious inheritance in the saints." (Ephesians 1:17-18)*

John received the revelation from the Lord and Jesus appeared to Him and spoke to him about what is going to happen in the future. *"The revelation of Jesus Christ, which God gave him to show his servants what must soon take place. He made it known by sending his angel to his servant John, who testifies to everything he saw — that is, the word of God and the testimony of Jesus Christ. Blessed is the one who reads the words of this prophecy, and blessed are those who hear it and take to heart what is written in it, because the time is near." (Revelation 1:1-3)*

God communicates with us in order for us to understand His plans and what's going to happen in the future. It's good that Jesus communicated with John so that we have the written word.

14. Silence

Our mind is cluttered when we don't know how to practice silence. God doesn't always talk but He wants us to be silent and wait so we can hear when He speaks to us. The more you practice clearing your mind and practice silence, the more you can recognize God's voice. While you are waiting, you may be able to tell that though there are no words spoken, God's presence can be felt in the silence. *"'Be still, and know that I am God; I will be exalted among the nations, I will be exalted in the earth.' The LORD Almighty is with us; the God of Jacob is our fortress. Selah"* (Psalm 46:10-11)

15. Nature

God communicates His presence through nature — thunder, lightning, thick clouds, smoke, and fire, etc. People trembled in fear when God's presence was shown to them through nature. *"On the morning of the third day there was thunder and lightning, with a thick cloud over the mountain, and a very loud trumpet blast. Everyone in the camp trembled. Then Moses led the people out of the camp to meet with God, and they stood at the foot of the mountain. Mount Sinai was covered with smoke, because the LORD descended on it in fire. The smoke billowed up from it like smoke from a furnace, the whole mountain trembled violently, and the sound of the trumpet grew louder and louder. Then Moses spoke and the voice of God answered him."* (Exodus 19:16-19)

The beauty of nature also speaks of the Creator's glory.

16. Signs and wonders

God showed the Israelites great signs and wonders while the Lord was leading them out of bondage from slavery. *"Ask now about the former days, long before your time, from the day God created man on the earth; ask from one end of the heavens to the other. Has anything so great as this ever happened, or has anything like it ever been heard of? Has any other people heard the voice of God speaking out of fire, as you have, and lived? Has any god ever tried to take for himself one nation out of another nation, by testings, by miraculous signs and wonders, by war, by a mighty hand and an outstretched arm, or by great and awesome deeds, like all the things the LORD your God did for you in Egypt before your very eyes? You were shown these things so that you might know that the LORD is God; besides him there is no other. From heaven he made you hear his voice to discipline you. On earth he showed you his great fire, and you heard his words from out of the fire."* (Deuteronomy 4:32-36)

Just as the Lord helped the Israelites, so also God frees people now from spiritual bondage through Jesus today. *"The Spirit of the Lord is on me, because he has anointed me to preach good news to the poor. He has sent me to proclaim freedom for the prisoners and recovery of sight for the blind, to release the oppressed, to proclaim the year of the Lord's favor."* (Luke 4:18-19)

This Scripture is not just for Jesus, but all the believers of Jesus. How can anyone free people from the bondage of spiritual prison? Jesus is still doing it, as well as through His workers, whom the Holy Spirit frees from spiritual prison.

17. An animal

When we are living in sin, God can use anyone to correct us, even animals. This is a rare case in the Bible and only one person had that experience. So far I haven't heard of anyone who said that God spoke to them through animals but Peter wrote about a prophet who heard God's message from a donkey. *"But he was rebuked for his wrongdoing by a donkey — a beast without speech — who spoke with a man's voice and restrained the prophet's madness." (2 Peter 2:16)*

"When the donkey saw the angel of the LORD standing in the road with a drawn sword in his hand, she turned off the road into a field. Balaam beat her to get her back on the road. Then the angel of the LORD stood in a narrow path between two vineyards, with walls on both sides. When the donkey saw the angel of the LORD, she pressed close to the wall, crushing Balaam's foot against it. So he beat her again. Then the angel of the LORD moved on ahead and stood in a narrow place where there was no room to turn, either to the right or to the left. When the donkey saw the angel of the LORD, she lay down under Balaam, and he was angry and beat her with his staff. Then the LORD opened the donkey's mouth, and she said to Balaam, 'What have I done to you to make you beat me these three times?' Balaam answered the donkey, 'You have made a fool of me! If I had a sword in my hand, I would kill you right now.' The donkey said to Balaam, 'Am I not your own donkey, which you have always ridden, to this day? Have I been in the habit of doing this to you?' 'No,' he said. Then the LORD opened Balaam's eyes, and he saw the angel of the LORD standing in the road with his sword drawn. So he bowed low and fell facedown. The angel of the LORD asked him, 'Why have you beaten your donkey these three times? I have come here to oppose you because your path is a reckless one before me. The donkey saw me and turned away from me these three times. If she had not turned away, I would certainly have killed you by now, but I would have spared her.' Balaam said to the angel of the LORD, 'I have sinned. I did not realize you were standing in the road to oppose me. Now if you are displeased, I will go

back." (Numbers 22:23-34)

18. Circumstances

God speaks to us through our circumstances. Sometimes God will close one door and open other doors. If you are listening to the Lord, you will know it before the door closes. Therefore, it's very important for you to practice listening. If people learn to pay attention to the Holy Spirit who can guide, He will prepare their hearts. They don't have to be in turmoil but accept the event and quickly move on.

Paul's mission trip was directed by the Holy Spirit and sometimes the doors didn't open. He recognized that the Holy Spirit was not letting them go to certain places because God had different plans for them.

Paul wrote, *"When they came to the border of Mysia, they tried to enter Bithynia, but the Spirit of Jesus would not allow them to. So they passed by Mysia and went down to Troas. During the night Paul had a vision of a man of Macedonia standing and begging him, 'Come over to Macedonia and help us.' After Paul had seen the vision, we got ready at once to leave for Macedonia, concluding that God had called us to preach the gospel to them." (Acts 16:7-10)*

Sometimes the Holy Spirit leads us to do something different than we have planned. We can be more effective when we listen to God and understand how God can lead us through our circumstances.

Sometimes our hardships in life are caused by our sinful nature and the display of our bad character. Even if we are careful, we are not always shielded from all the bad things in life because other people make mistakes. That's a part of living in a world with other imperfect people in an imperfect world. Many times people hurt people. We hurt ourselves and others. When we put ourselves in a bad situation with people who lack good character and morals, we will get hurt. Paul warns us, *"Do not be misled: 'Bad company corrupts good character.' Come back to your senses as you ought, and stop sinning; for there are some who are ignorant of God — I say this to your shame." (1 Corinthians 15:33-34)*

Paul wrote, *"For all have sinned and fall short of the glory of God." (Romans 3:23)* Don't blame God for other people's sinful, selfish actions or your lack of godly behaviors. We need to take the responsibility and learn not to blame God for our shortcomings.

19. Spiritual gifts

Have you wondered how some people are so knowledgeable or have such spiritual wisdom? That's because the Holy Spirit has given them the gift to share with others. All these gifts are freely given from God and we can learn from others who have received those gifts.

Paul explains this way: *"To one there is given through the Spirit the message of wisdom, to another the message of knowledge by means of the same Spirit, to another faith by the same Spirit, to another gifts of healing by that one Spirit, to another miraculous powers, to another prophecy, to another distinguishing between spirits, to another speaking in different kinds of tongues, and to still another the interpretation of tongues. All these are the work of one and the same Spirit, and he gives them to each one, just as he determines.'" (1 Corinthians 12:8-11)*

20. Other people

When David first committed the sin of adultery, he should have repented, and asked God for advice about how he could clean up the mess he had made. Instead, he made his own plan to cover up his sin by murdering Uriah. *"After the time of mourning was over, David had her brought to his house, and she became his wife and bore him a son. But the thing David had done displeased the LORD."* (2 Samuel 11:27) *"The LORD sent Nathan to David."* (2 Samuel 12:1a)

God spoke to David many times but this time God wouldn't even speak to David directly. The Lord sent Nathan, the prophet, to confront David's sin and he repented.

This Scripture teaches us that, when we live in sin, our communication with God can break down. If you live in sin, you may be justifying your sin. Other mature Christians who know the Scriptures can tell you that you need to shape up. When other people like your family, relatives or friends start telling you the same thing, that you need to make changes, go to God and ask Him for wisdom if you have something that you need to repent or to change. See if there is anything you are doing that is not pleasing to the Lord, God may not talk to you directly but speak through other people.

God can speak to us with confirmation and encouragement through other people when He is pleased with us. It's important to listen to the Lord so you can be encouraged by Him.

Moses' father-in-law suggested that Moses seek others to help him and he did. *(Exodus 18:13-16)* We need the help of other spiritually mature people in making sound decisions. In the process, we will be able to serve the Lord more effectively.

21. Inspirational writings

Did you know that the Holy Spirit can speak to you through other people's testimonies and inspirational writings? If the writer is anointed and led by the Holy Spirit, what you read will be a blessing and you will be touched by it. Actually that's what the Bible is about. The Holy Spirit led people to write the stories of how the Lord led people.

When we read the Bible, inspirational writings and testimonies, the Holy Spirit can reveal the meaning of the story to us, so we can learn about God through other people's stories.

In fact, our testimony is not just our story, but also God's story of how He has helped us. That's why it is powerful and gives us hope that God can do so much more than we can think or imagine.

God is continuously blessing people with the Holy Spirit and encouraging people to write, so they can bless others through sharing their testimonies. Our testimony about how God leads us, blesses us and heals us is a powerful message of hope for others. God can use our stories of tears to bring healing.

Why do people cry while they read books? Somehow they were touched by the story. The anointed stories can bring healing in our hearts. It can bring tears, deep conviction and understanding.

You don't need to be surprised when you are crying and deep understanding comes. The tears bring healing to your heart and it's the work of the Holy Spirit. At times we don't realize which areas need healing, but the Holy Spirit does.

The books written by human knowledge and

wisdom don't have this anointing but may give you some knowledge and information. The books and writings anointed by the Holy Spirit could bring healing to our mind and heart.

You might hear the Holy Spirit's voice giving you clear directions about what you need to do at the moment that you are touched by the story. The Holy Spirit is speaking to you. Other people's spiritual experiences with the Lord can make a tremendous difference and will help us grow in our relationship with the Lord.

22. Inspirational music

Have you been touched by inspirational music? Often tears will well up in your eyes that bring a better understanding of God's love. God can speak to us through music that is anointed by the Holy Spirit. When people write songs which are led by the Holy Spirit, those songs speak to our heart and we hear good voices from the Lord.

Pastor Sun Hui East of First Love Harvest Church gave me the best advice. She told me that the worship songs had to be anointed and the preacher has to be anointed in order for the congregation to experience the Holy Spirit. I learned to rely on the Holy Spirit's leading in worship as to which song I should play. I pray for God's leading in my ministry and pray for anointing of the Holy Spirit so He can speak and bring healing to people who attend worship services.

23. Inspirational art

God created the universe and everything in it. He is creative and we are created in the image of God. We have inherited that creativity, the desire to create something. God designed Noah's ark and the Ark of the Covenant. He tells people to build and inspires certain people to create art to glorify the Lord and to tell the world about His greatness. He speaks to us through the artists who are dedicated to the Lord and uses their gifts to remind us about God so we can get to know Him.

Once I was in New York to attend a pastor's retreat and visited a big chapel which had all different types of art work and expressions of Christ from different countries. On top of the ceiling was a huge drawing of Christ. That was one of the most awesome pictures of Jesus I have ever seen. That gave me chills. I felt the presence of the Lord. That was one experience I will never forget. God can speak to us through people's art work.

24. Tears

God speaks to us through our tears. I am not talking about tears when we are upset or angry. These are coming from our flesh and sometimes they are not helpful. I am talking about tears that come when the Lord gives us understanding. Sometimes we don't even understand why we cry, but deep in our heart we are touched by God.

These kinds of tears are like watering a dried garden. As we weep before God, He brings healing. He is sharing His heart and purifying us through tears.

In the book of Hosea, God compares our hearts to a garden. *"Judah must plow, and Jacob must break up the ground. Sow for yourselves righteousness, reap the fruit of unfailing love, and break up your unplowed ground; for it is time to seek the Lord, until he comes and showers righteousness on you. But you have planted wickedness, you have reaped evil, you have eaten the fruit of deception." (Hosea 10:11b-13a)*

He blesses us with showers of tears as we spend time with Him. The Holy Spirit starts breaking the hard ground of our hearts. Sometimes we are grieving for our sins or others. As we weep, the Lord brings us comfort and healing and purifies us. Tears are special gifts from the Lord in this case.

When we worship the Lord individually or with others, God often appears and people are overwhelmed with the presence of the Lord and tears come. God may have some message to speak to us and we understand what He wants to say. Our love for the Lord grows. Our confidence and faith in the Lord grows.

Chapter 8

The Stages of Listening

1. Feel nothing stage

You don't feel anything when you pray. You are not sure if God is listening to your prayers. You even try to pretend that God is listening when you pray, but you are not sure if He is really listening to you.

2. Feel you are missing something

You feel God is far away and you are not sure if He is listening or not. You know something is missing in your life. You feel God is not answering your prayers. You are beginning to understand that there is something lacking in your life, and you are not quite sure what that is. Don't give up at this stage. Keep praying and spend time with the Lord and you will eventually understand the presence of the Lord. You will know He is right there with you listening to your prayer. Start reading the Gospels to get to know Jesus and this will help you sharpen your spiritual senses.

3. Understanding what is missing

You begin to understand what is missing. People may feel that there is something more to a relationship with God but they don't know how to have that experience or relationship. This is an agonizing stage for many people. They have the longing to know God more than ever, their desire to listen to God's voice grows. They may want to receive signs from the Lord that He is real, but it seems God is silent.

When nothing seems to satisfy their request, some people may think that God is not real or that He doesn't care because He doesn't speak to them.

Many people don't have much patience and don't understand that this is a spiritual quest that we are called to pursue if we want to find Him. *"You will seek me and find me when you seek me with all your heart." (Jeremiah 29:13)*

Start by reading the Bible and listen to the Word of God. He speaks to our hearts with His word. Ask the Holy Spirit to give you clear understanding of what is missing in your life. God knows how to get our attention by informing our spiritual senses when we are missing something.

Read the book of Revelation chapter one through chapter three to understand how Jesus evaluates different spiritual leaders' spiritual condition. See if any of the letters speak to your heart.

4. You learn to wait and listen

You feel God is silent. Your thoughts are clearer than before. You feel close to the Lord even though you may not hear anything. God wants you to listen and wait. If you can be patient and wait in silence, you will have a breakthrough in hearing God's voice in your heart. He can speak to us with or without words. Timing is in God's hands, but you have to have the desire and the heart to listen and wait. Those who are earnestly seeking God for a relationship will be rewarded eventually. Be persistent in waiting and know that you are in the presence of the Lord whenever you go to God in prayer.

5. Beginning to understand God's voice

You are amazed that God can speak to your heart and you are filled with gratitude. You understand God's heart with or without words. You will understand assignments that God gives you. He may be asking you to do something you don't want to do. You end up debating with God why you don't want to obey Him and you come up with many excuses.

Whether it is repenting, forgiving, or training to learn more about God, it becomes clear to you. You know this and understand that the assignment is not what you have thought about or wanted to do, it's coming from somewhere else. God may be asking you for a closer relationship. You are to answer the call to grow spiritually. If you start obeying the Lord's assignment, you can go into the next stage where God will be leading your life and ministry.

6. You have conversations with the Lord

You ask the Lord and you hear His response immediately. You have developed a relationship with the Holy Spirit. Your confidence in God has grown and you know He hears you and He responds to you.

You feel comfortable waiting in silence. You have learned that the Lord is silent at times so you can seek Him. You will be learning how to be humble before the Lord as you start understanding the deep thoughts of God. He will start to share things that you never even expected to know or think or imagine. You will understand God has so much to offer in your loving relationship with Him.

Your desire to love the Lord and willingness to do

what He is asking of you grows. This is a loving relationship which we all need to seek and cherish. Loving the Lord with all our heart, mind, soul, and strength will become your first priority.

At this stage, when you fail to obey the Lord, you will understand immediately and feel remorse. You have learned to feel and sense the Holy Spirit's grief and pain.

Your relationship with the Lord and understanding His heart will lead you to serve others who are hurting. You will understand how much the Lord cares about others who are suffering and are in pain without knowing Christ. You will break down at times when you feel the pain of others. You will understand that God understands their pain as well. You are motivated to help others because you love God and you understand other people's pain.

You will not have much heart for the worldly desires anymore. You have found the purpose and meaning in loving the Lord and serving the Lord. Your joy and peace is the evidence of the Holy Spirit working in your life.

Chapter 9

Questions and Answers

1. How do I get to know God better so I can hear Him?

Consider doing the following spiritual exercises: Read the Bible 30 minutes a day. Or read one gospel a day to get to know Jesus for the next 30 days. As you get to know the heart of Jesus, you will understand how He will speak to you. Ask the Holy Spirit to give you wisdom to understand the Word of God. You can gain spiritual wisdom. Keep spending time with the Lord. Read the Bible throughout the day and you will get to know him.

Avoid distractions in life. Distraction is anything that hinders your relationship with God. Learn to cut off worldly entertainments and ungodly conversations with others. Practice listening in silence, you will get to know the Holy Spirit's small voice speaking to your heart.

2. Is there a certain prayer or anything else I have to do before I can hear God speak to me?

Practice silence and try to listen to God's voice. Many people's hearts are filled with many thoughts and are overwhelmed. You need to cleanse your heart with the help of the Holy Spirit so you will recognize His voice. If you have not learned to recognize God's voice, there is a chance that He has been speaking to you in many ways, but you may not have recognized it. If you haven't really heard God speaking to your heart, then you need to practice listening.

Prayer: "Holy Spirit, help me to understand what you are trying to say. Is there anything that I need to repent of or make changes to? Is there anyone I need to forgive? Is there any ungodly habit that I need to change? Please help me to recognize it and give me wisdom and an obedient heart to follow you."

God speaks in many different ways and the Bible is one way God speaks to us, so keep reading. You need to practice silence while waiting so you can clear your mind and listen to the small voice of the Holy Spirit.

3. How do I listen to God's voice in my dreams?

Whenever you have a dream, write it down and ask God for the interpretation. Sometimes God gives us the interpretation in our dreams. However, I do not believe all the dreams are from God. Sometimes people suffer from nightmares. That is not coming from the Lord. It's a tormenting spirit, which causes pain. You have to be patient and wait. Be persistent, He may speak to you by giving you Scriptures, or understanding comes to you.

4. How do we really know God is listening?

You have to have faith that God can hear your prayers. He is God. He is not like a person with limitations. He can not only hear the words you are praying, but He also knows and understands all your thoughts, intentions and motivations.

David had that knowledge and he describes it in Psalm 139. I encourage you to read it. He wrote, "*O LORD, you have searched me and you know me. You know when I sit and when I rise; you perceive my thoughts from afar.*

You discern my going out and my lying down; you are familiar with all my ways. Before a word is on my tongue you know it completely, O LORD. You hem me in-behind and before; you have laid your hand upon me. Such knowledge is too wonderful for me, too lofty for me to attain. Where can I go from your Spirit? Where can I flee from your presence?" (Psalm 139:1-7)

The Bible says God hears our prayers. As you get to know God and spend lots of time in prayer, you will sense that God is hearing your prayers. Your spirit feels and knows it. If you sense that God is not listening, that means that there is something that you have between you and God. You need to find out if there is anything that you are not obeying.

Listen and see what God is asking you to do and obey Him. Then you will feel God's peace and loving presence even in the midst of turmoil and pain that you may be going through.

He is listening and the sooner you recognize and do things to repair your relationship, the sooner you will find peace and joy. There may be a time that if you are not sensitive to the Holy Spirit, your prayer may not be pleasing the Lord. That, too, God will reveal to you as you develop a close relationship with the Holy Spirit.

5. How do I know that God is going to answer my prayers?

God hears your prayers and He will answer according to His will, in His time. If you are continuously reading the Bible and praying, developing a close relationship with the Lord, He will tell you if you will get what you asked for or not. When he says no, you need to change your prayers. When He says yes, you can start praising God for answering your prayers even before you see it.

It's a relationship and how much time you spend with the Lord and how much you are paying attention to His voice will make a difference. He will speak to the people who seek Him. Be patient. Your persistence in praying will get an answer.

<u>6. I am confused when I pray in the sense that I want to be hopeful and optimistic about the future, but maybe what I pray for is not God's will. Maybe He has something else in mind</u>.

James talks about why people don't get what they want: Either not praying or praying for the wrong things.

James wrote, *"What causes fights and quarrels among you? Don't they come from your desires that battle within you? You want something, but don't get it. You kill and covet, but you cannot have what you want. You quarrel and fight. You do not have, because you do not ask God. When you ask, you do not receive, because you ask with wrong motives that you may spend what you get on your pleasures. You adulterous people, don't you know that friendship with the world is hatred toward God? Anyone who chooses to be a friend of the world becomes an enemy of God. Or do you think Scripture says without reason that the spirit he caused to live in us envies intensely? But he gives us more grace. That is why Scripture says: "God opposes the proud but gives grace to the humble." (James 4:1-6)*

You need to know what you are asking for. Is your request pleasing and beneficial to God's kingdom? Or is your prayer selfish and if it is given, will you fall into sin? All these questions are important to know if your prayer is going to be answered or not. When we pray for something to use for our sinful desires, God is not going to give it to us.

If you have restless feelings when you request something, the Holy Spirit may be telling you that your prayer is not going to be answered as you requested. If you learn to listen to the voice of the Holy Spirit, you will know if your prayer is what God wants. If it's coming from your own desires, you may feel confused. Spend more time in reading the Bible to find out if what you are asking is God's will or not.

7. How to keep on listening without being interrupted by other things or things people say. How do I focus when so many things run through my head?

There are times when we have to pay attention to what is going on around us and we cannot ignore them. That is a part of living. You need to find a way to spend time alone with God. Getting up early and praying is a good time with no interruptions for some people. Or you can spend time in prayer and meditation after everyone goes to sleep, if you can stay up late.

You need to make an effort to focus on the Lord. Develop a habit of praying as you walk, to focus your mind on the Lord. Learn to clear your mind, and ask the Lord to speak to you by saying, "Lord Jesus, speak to me, I am listening."

You may have to ask others to be quiet, while you read the Bible and meditate. You can start to memorize the short verses in the Scriptures to keep focus on the Lord. You can quietly recite *Psalm 23* or *Luke 4:18-19* or your favorite Scriptures which can calm your heart and then pray, "Lord Jesus, I am listening. If there is anything you would like to say to me, please speak to me."

Then clear your mind and try to hear what He would say. The more you practice silence, the better you will be able to listen and hear the small voice of God.

8. When I pray, I try to hear God's voice and I feel He does not talk to me. Why?

God doesn't speak to us all the time. He is saying that you need to be attentive and listen, but don't worry. He hears you and He is going to answer you in His way and in His time.

Interestingly, in the book of Revelation, there is silence in heaven for about 30 minutes. During that time John saw the angels work. *"When he opened the seventh seal, there was silence in heaven for about half an hour. And I saw the seven angels who stand before God, and to them were given seven trumpets. Another angel, who had a golden censer, came and stood at the altar. He was given much incense to offer, with the prayers of all the saints, on the golden altar before the throne. The smoke of the incense, together with the prayers of the saints, went up before God from the angel's hand." (Revelation 8:1-4)* So, there is a processing time in our prayers.

You will develop a listening ear as a child learns how to walk. So, be patient in waiting but don't give up. If you wait long enough the Holy Spirit will clearly speak to you at some point.

I ask people to count the days when they start the practice of listening. Depending on how much you are aware of how God speaks to you. The voice you will hear in your heart with words or without words, will transform your life. So, keep waiting in silence and obey when God asks you to take care of business that will clean up your life. That's how God speaks to us many times. We have so much to clean up in our lives.

As you grow more in the knowledge of the Scriptures, you will hear more clearly of what God is trying to say to you. Like a little baby who eventually understands what his/her parents are saying. Keep reading the Bible, it will help you become familiar with the heavenly Father's language and you will understand what He is trying to say to you.

9. I don't know what God wants me to do with my life. How can I hear it from Him?

You need to understand that God has already given the basic formula of showing us what we should do with our life. The most important thing is to love the Lord with all your heart, mind, soul, and strength. Then you should love your neighbor as yourself. To love your neighbors, you have to love yourself.

How we show our love for God and our neighbors is to be a witness for Christ by reaching out to others who are in need of Christ and help them who are poor and hurting. Saving souls and teaching others to grow so they can obey the Lord. That is Jesus' commandment.

The Holy Spirit has given us many gifts so we can build up the body of Christ. Find out what your gifts are and try to use them to win souls for Christ. Teach others so they can grow spiritually. People can do this in many ways by sharing their testimony or making music or writing books or through media.

Everyone receives spiritual gifts or talents from God. We can use them to serve the Lord by serving others. God can speak to us through other people. Some are reaching out to the homeless or prisoners or church congregations. You need to ask the Lord to give you understanding of what you should do to serve the Lord. As you wait for an answer from the Lord, instead of sitting and waiting, start exploring different ministry opportunities. As you serve the Lord in different settings, the Holy Spirit will reveal to you if that is your calling or not. Our calling is related to our gifts. When we use our gifts, we will be effective and fruitful. Ask the Lord to open the doors for you to use your gifts to the maximum to serve the Lord. Keep praying and ask him as you serve where you should be.

In addition, find some mature Christians who can mentor you and give you some guidance on how to serve the Lord. As you serve, if you have restless feelings and you are feeling empty and unhappy, the Holy Spirit may be telling you that you are not using your gifts to the maximum. Ask the Lord to give you wisdom to find the right ministry in the right place.

10. How do I know when it's God's voice and not just my own thoughts? I want to hear God's voice so badly. I'm not sure if it's just my own thoughts trying to make me believe I am hearing from God.

You need to learn to discern four different voices in your mind: 1) Your voice; 2) Other people's voices; 3) The devil's voice; 4) The Holy Spirit's voice. What you need to do is evaluate your thoughts or the voices that come to your mind. If it is the devil's voice, he will try to make you fall into sin, despair, discouragement and turmoil. The Holy Spirit will reveal to us our sins so we can learn not to fall into them.

The Holy Spirit will tell you to do something to grow in faith or help others to grow in faith, like, "Go and pray instead of watching TV" or "Go and read the Scriptures" or "Talk to someone to share Christ." In any case, if you listen to the devil, you will fall into sin or sadness and depressing thoughts. If you obey the Holy Spirit, you will grow in faith and you can help others to grow in faith.

Your voice is trying to figure out what you need to do with those thoughts. Other voices are from our memories or what we hear. If you are not sure, you need to spend time reading the Bible more and pray more. Practice listening in silence as you pray. When God speaks to you, you will recognize it. It will come with conviction.

God speaks to us in many ways. The Holy Spirit can speak to our hearts with words or without words. Conviction of sin is God speaking to you clearly saying that you have sinned and need to repent and make changes in your life. Even though you may think you have the knowledge of your sins, we cannot see ourselves clearly unless the Holy Spirit reveals them to you. The voice of conviction of sins you have not repented is from the Lord. As you spend more time praying and listening, the voices will become clearer and you will understand the origin of the voices.

You don't have peace if you are doing something that God is not pleased with. If you have heard a voice in your mind and you don't know whose voice it is, that means you haven't learned to distinguish the origin of the voices. Read the Bible and ask God for wisdom.

11. How do I talk to God and keep him in my life every day?

Talk to Jesus in the following manner and be creative in talking to Him:

(1) Talk to Him with all respect and reverence.

(2) Talk to Him as if you are talking to a loving father who loves you deeply. Worship Him in songs and praises. That is talking to God.

(3) Talk to Him as if you are talking to a friend who cares deeply to the point that they will do anything for you.

(4) Talk to Him as if you are one of His family members and he is looking after you.

(5) Talk to Him about all your concerns, worries, fears and desires. He understands everyone's thoughts, even though you may not hear anything.

(6) Talk to Him about how much you love and care for Him.

(7) Talk to Him about all your needs for wisdom, knowledge, understanding and revelation so you will know the spiritual truth and what God wants you to do with your life.

(8) Talk to Him if you need direction in different matters. In other words, talk to God about whatever you have in mind. But if you only talk to him when you have problems, you miss out on listening to His heart and the directions that He wants to give you. So, practice listening to God's voice half of the time and only talk half of the time. You can have conversations instead of acting like you are talking to an answering machine.

(9) Thank God for everything. Praise Him and honor the Lord. When the Lord is ready to speak to you, He will speak to you.

12. Why do people have a difficult time recognizing or hearing God's voice?

We have many misconceptions about how God speaks to us. We try to understand God with our own experiences. Some reasons why people have a difficult time are:

(1) <u>We treat God like an answering machine</u>: Some prayers are a one-way conversation. I was in this condition for a long time, but I am glad that God taught me to listen.

(2) <u>Expect nothing from the Lord</u>: People don't expect to hear from the Lord. Even if God speaks to them, these people don't consider that He will speak to them so they ignore the voice of God.

(3) <u>Department Store relationship</u>: Some people give orders to God. When they don't get what they asked for, they are upset or angry and they don't want anything to do with Him.

(4) <u>God wouldn't listen to little things</u>: Some people don't bother to ask God anything or try to communicate with God because they think God would not listen to trivial things. They don't expect anything from God and they don't try to understand how He speaks to them.

(5) <u>God won't speak to us</u>: The Scripture teaches us that God speaks to people. *"The Mighty One, God, the LORD, speaks and summons the earth from the rising of the sun to the place where it sets. From Zion, perfect in beauty, God shines forth. Our God comes and will not be silent; a fire devours before him, and around him a tempest rages. He summons the heavens above, and the earth, that he may*

judge his people: 'Gather to me my consecrated ones, who made a covenant with me by sacrifice.' And the heavens proclaim his righteousness, for God himself is judge. Selah 'Hear, O my people, and I will speak, O Israel, and I will testify against you: I am God, your God.'" (Psalm 50:1-7)

(6) <u>When we live in sin, God is not happy with us</u>: The Lord may not speak to us until we clean up our lives and repent. God would be more willing to talk to people who are humbling themselves by praying, seeking God and repenting. *"If my people, who are called by my name, will humble themselves and pray and seek my face and turn from their wicked ways, then will I hear from heaven and will forgive their sin and will heal their land. Now my eyes will be open and my ears attentive to the prayers offered in this place." (2 Chronicles 7:14-15)*

(7) <u>We ask for the wrong things</u>: James tells us not to expect God to answer our prayers when we want to use it for our own sinful desires. *"When you ask, you do not receive, because you ask with wrong motives, that you may spend what you get on your pleasures. You adulterous people, don't you know that friendship with the world is hatred toward God? Anyone who chooses to be a friend of the world becomes an enemy of God." (James 4:3-4)*

(8) <u>Misunderstood relationship</u>: People think God only spoke during the biblical times and He will not speak to us. Jesus promised that the Holy Spirit will be with us and speak to us about Him. The Holy Spirit will guide, direct, teach, comfort, and counsel us. *"But when he, the Spirit of truth, comes, he will guide you into all truth. He will not speak on his own; he will speak only what he hears, and he will tell you what is yet to come. He will bring glory to me by taking from what is mine and making it known to you." (John 16:13-14)*

(9) <u>Lack of encouragement to listen</u>: People are not encouraged to listen or recognize God's voice. They are not taught to listen. Many are encouraged to pray which means talk to God but we have not been taught to listen to God's voice. We need to learn to be silent before the Lord so He can speak to us. God grieves when we don't pay attention to Him.

(10) <u>Do not understand how God speaks to people</u>: God may already be speaking to people with many languages but they do not realize or know how to recognize them.

(11) <u>They may not know how to discern voices</u>: We hear many voices and we need to have discernment to know which is God's voice.

Chapter 10

I Heard The Voice

1. "I HEARD THE VOICE" by Marvin Vicks

I became a believer of the Lord at the age of 13 and attended church. I had been struggling with faith all of my life. I was going through many problems and I would pray and ask for help. It seemed that there was no response to my prayers.

Then one day, my friend and I went to Wendy's restaurant and picked up some food. We stopped at the stop light and I started eating a baked potato. As I swallowed it, I began to choke. I couldn't breathe and couldn't talk. I was looking up to my friend who was the driver and I pointed at my back so he could hit me to make me breathe. He couldn't understand what I was doing and just looked at me. I got so hot I took off my shirt, opened the passenger side door and got out. I stood up, holding on to the back of the car because I felt faint.

I looked toward the traffic for help, but I couldn't talk so I couldn't ask for help. My friend who couldn't understand just looked at me. I leaned over the truck. At that moment, I prayed to the Lord in my mind, "Lord, help me." Immediately, within seconds, I felt the air being blown into my lung, I began breathing. My heart was pounding fast which meant I was able to breathe.

I forgot about this incident for a long time. Then ten years later, my wife and I got into a fight. She got angry, reached down to the floor, got a buck knife and swung at me. My neighbors called the police. Even though I didn't press charges against my wife, the police took her to jail.

Later that night, my wife's son, 12 or 13 years old, called me and said he got into trouble and I needed to pick him up from his home. My car didn't work so I walked. As I was walking along, I began to talk to myself. "So many bad things have happened in my life. If there is a God, He has never answered any of my prayers." Five to ten minutes later, I heard a loud clear voice in my mind, "Hold up, wait a minute. Oh, yes, I did answer one of your prayers. I heard your prayer when you couldn't breathe." I stopped walking and looked everywhere. There was no one. I wanted to see if others heard what I just had heard.

I started running because of what I had heard, then stopped, and started laughing to myself. "That's right. I forgot about that Lord. I should shut my mouth before something else happens to me." When I heard God's voice, I was not on any drugs or alcohol. I heard the loud voice in my mind, so clear, that I will never forget what I heard that day.

I told my wife about it and she said, "It's the Lord talking to you." I told my uncle who is a minister, and he asked me to visit his church to share my testimony about how God spoke to me.

When I get depressed or worried and feel there is nothing out there to help me, I remember this experience. It encourages me and builds my faith back up. I shared this story with my celly and with others throughout my life. I know God still speaks to people. I am not special but God used me to deliver this message. The message is to keep your faith and hold on; deliverance will come when you least expect it.

2. "I CRIED OUT TO GOD" by Laylay Manuel

I was born and raised in a Christian family. I have eight brothers and six sisters. I am 19 years old. They say age isn't anything but a number. Well, here that's the case. I get told a lot that I am young and I haven't lived life yet because I always say I am ready to be with my Father. I say that because this life is so hard to live and brings suffering and pain. Here is my testimony. At seven years old, I started running away from home, hanging out with the mafia. They showed me a love I wasn't getting at home. I was doing lines, smoking weed, drinking, popping pills, learning how to have a cold heart and how to pull a trigger.

I was rebellious toward my family and didn't want them to start caring because they never did unless I was in trouble. I hung out with the big boys until age 13. I fought a lot and thought I was bad. I got stuck on heroin at age 14. One day while I was completely wacked out of my mind, I slipped out of consciousness. When I opened my eyes, I felt my flesh melting. I started walking, I heard screams, crying, and was in pain all over.

After how long, I don't know, I realized I wasn't as bad as I thought. I cried out to God. I didn't want to be in this place of pain, sorrow and grief. I couldn't do it. I called out and almost immediately a hand was extended down to me, a voice so powerful yet so gentle said, "Take my hand. You have a matter of seconds before this becomes you."

I grabbed the hand and I was brought to a room

walking by the most beautiful person dressed in white. I mean white that was whiter than snow. I was in harmony. My burdens all disappeared. I was happy. I looked at a screen. I was in a hospital room laid out on a bed.

The doctor and my family gathered around me. I heard the doctor say, "It's been three days, I can't hold her any longer." He pronounced me dead. Seeing my family cry like that, especially my mom, tore my heart.

I looked at the man next to me. I told him, "Please don't take me away from my family. I will do right, please." I fell at his feet, begging and crying a river. A hand as gentle as a feather laid on my back. I was brought back to my human body with a shake.

The doctor didn't know what to say. My vitals were strong and healthy. I went home that day. There are a select few who witnessed this in the hospital. God showed me the way I was headed. I am here to say to all that hell is as real as heaven. I am a witness. I am currently involved in the choir and children's ministry. I am loving every minute of it.

If you are heading down that road, beware. Hell is full of pain, grief, sorrow and torment. I was a child seeking love that was never given, but I realized I will always have love from my Father above.

I am currently detached from my family but I have their support. When I need them, they are there. I am happily married to the love of my life. He gives me more than I can ask for. He is my angel. I also have three wonderful kids I adore and I try to give them what I never had. I have found my happiness. I say to all He is coming soon! Heaven is as real as hell. I've seen it and witnessed the miracles God can do. I was a child: *"When I was a child, I talked like a child. I thought like a child, I reasoned like a child. When I became a man, I put childish ways behind me."* (1 Corinthians 13:11)

3. "HE SPOKE TO ME" by Dee Anderson

From the start I volunteered quickly, having no idea what I had gotten myself into. Not quite what I had expected, but definitely not something I regret either. Chaplain McDonald came and spoke to me about writing another story for yet another book. I didn't hesitate one bit. Little did I know it was the Holy Spirit speaking through me. Then I sat down to write and didn't have a clue where to start or even how, I sat bewildered by the fact that I volunteered so quickly with so little of a clue of what to write.

The Chaplain and I had not yet discussed that I hadn't a clue on what to write, but the Holy Spirit must have spoken to her because she came to me about my problem. She spoke to me about prayer and letting God lead my story and so we prayed and after prayer, I mentioned to her about how before I even told her I was having difficulty on what to write, she already knew. The Chaplain has offered me great insight and wisdom on my writings and God uses her to speak to me with a magnificent power unlike anything I have ever experienced before.

So here is another one of my stories. I hope it touches many. I have recently been having a lot of difficulties and complications with my case. For four months I have sat in Adams County receiving no guidance or representation from my attorney. He had missed almost all of my court dates and has yet to come visit me except for like two times. Both the times he visited he brought the same news of my offer from my plea being 10-16 years in prison. Not an easy thing to swallow, nor did it sit well on my shoulders.

Time was passing and the court date for my motions was coming up soon. I began getting worried and soon started to fill up with doubt in my mind and my heart. Worry led to doubt and doubt led to an emptiness. My heart was heavy and I started questioning God's love. I thought if God loved me, He would show me a light. The following Thursday which was August 18, 2011, I was awakened by the deputies telling me to pack it up. I had no idea where I was going but I knew I wasn't going home. I complied and within minutes soon found out I was going on a writ to Jefferson County. I was very excited but again had no idea what I was about to encounter or experience.

I arrived in Jeffco and was in a holding cell in booking with a girl named Amanda. We conversed about why we were in jail. She seemed to have little to no faith so I spoke to her about my understanding of a heroin addiction. Although I had never been addicted I understood the problems that came with it due to my mother being a heroin addict. I gave her insight on change for herself and for her child. I even prayed with her. We were soon sent to our housing unit in 4B.

We were greeted by a very friendly woman with blondish hair whom I did not know her name nor did she know mine. She got us our bedding and clothing. Amanda and I were placed in separate caves but we were directly next to each other, the only thing separating us was a wall. Neither of us said much of anything to anyone. That night as I lay close to the wall it seemed cold but as I prayed for Amanda and her healing of this terrible addiction and to send angels to comfort her I felt a warmth from the other side of the wall.

The following day the friendly woman with the blondish colored hair came to me and said, "The Holy Spirit spoke to me about you. He gave me a vision about you." I turned around to see who she was speaking to, but I found nobody around me. I was confused so I asked her what she was talking about. She said that the Holy Spirit came to her and told her that I was not going to serve time in prison, that I was being called to Victory Outreach to speak to people about gangs, violence, drug addiction and much more. She said I was going to be used by God to minister to many by using my story and sharing my experiences. I was dumbfounded and in complete shock, my jaw dropped with my mouth open wide and eyes huge.

Just one minute ago, I thought maybe this woman was pulling my leg. Now I knew this was the truth of the Holy Spirit speaking. I knew this because well for one this woman didn't know a thing about me. She didn't even know my name or what I was incarcerated for nor did she know anything I had been through. We hadn't even spoken yet. Somehow though the Holy Spirit spoke to her and let her know about me. I was stunned. I had no idea what to say so I nodded my head and walked away.

Everyday after she came to me about the Holy Spirit speaking to her and finally I asked her what her name was and why she was telling me all this, for she didn't even know me or my name, or what I had been through. She replied with a warm friendly laugh and smile saying, "Well, hi, I'm Debbie, no I did not know your name or why you are here or what you have done, but the Holy Spirit has been speaking to me about you. You have a calling from the Lord to help others. You have a gift." She then later invited me to a prayer circle and asked me to pray. I prayed and many girls cried and said they had chills, they said I prayed an amazing prayer that touched them. I received many hugs from everyone telling me how God spoke to them through me. I became close to many people in very little time, Debbie being one, specifically. I was very sad when I had to leave.

I came back to ACDF on a Thursday and that following Sunday I wrote and read my testimony. People who listened said I touched them. I reflected that night on my testimony. It was crazy that a few days prior to the reading of my testimony I was being told by a woman I didn't know nor did she know me that I would share my story to help others. Next thing you know, the chaplain was putting my testimony in a book that thousands would soon read. This was the beginning of the vision she had of me through the Holy Spirit.

I went on another writ to Jeffco shortly after that Sunday and I went straight from booking to Court. As I was coming out of court I ran into Debbie. She started crying immediately, so did I. We prayed and praised God. She told me everyone missed me and that I helped many. Another part of her vision came true already. Amanda, the girl I was in booking with the last time I came to Jeffco, was in good health and spirit. The Lord told me I helped her.

I prayed again in a prayer circle with the same

responses as last time. I was amazed! This woman of God was so right with everything she has said. I soon left Jeffco and came back to ACDF. Again I was so sad to leave my friends and other people.

The Chaplain then asked me to write this story about voices. I had no idea what to write so I prayed and the Holy Spirit spoke to me and lead me in this story about the good voices of God and other people.

The Holy Spirit has spoken to me with pureness through many people, especially through Debbie and Chaplain McDonald. I thank all those who have prayed for me and with me and I thank God for opening my heart and allowing me to share my story once again.

I pray for the healing of all who are hurting, I pray for people to open their heart and mind so that they may hear God's voice when He speaks to them. *Psalm 46:10* says, *"Be still, and know that I am God; I will be exalted among the nations, I will be exalted in the earth."* This will help many. If you are still, you will hear God's voice.

4. "UNCONDITIONAL LOVE" by Georgette Wires

I was sitting in the window, just looking and I heard, "You didn't deserve that." So, I was like, ok, and then I heard it again. When I realized what was said to me, a huge release began to melt in me and I just began to weep. They were tears of cleansing, not of anguish or sorrow. To me it was like Jesus saying, "I knew all about it. I understand your sufferings." Forever, I have been crippled with a mindset of "anything that happens to me I deserve it, whether I did it or it was being done to me."

As a little girl it was instilled in me that I was "bad" and I would never amount to anything. I'd always be a failure, never deserving anything good. As I grew, so did this verbal curse that had been spoken over my life that my father and many others told me all the while I was also being physically and sexually abused.

When you are told something for so long, repetition has a way of locking things in and eventually you will begin to act these things out. You believe it of yourself. Well not today, not anymore, not for me. Ironically, on the day of love, "Valentine's Day," this curse was broken and destroyed. Quietly, Jesus simply spoke to my heart and deliverance came.

What's so awesome about this experience is that I didn't realize how severe this curse had been. It crippled my mind and set numerous bondages that had been spoken over me and even placed upon me. There were even more bondages I had picked up over the years of my life.

Jesus and I have been on this journey a great while now — 17 years — and for me, I have been bound by the belief that I was unworthy. I was a failure. I had developed a paralyzing fear that I had continuously disappointed Jesus. I would still read my Bible and I would pray. Early on I had developed a love for Jesus and would always just want Him to love me back. Today I know my trust had been half-hearted as well as my belief concerning my relationship with Him and what I thought I deserved.

To know how to trust; to trust that He could really love someone like me, I didn't quite understand that His love was something that I couldn't earn. His love is genuine, everlasting, and totally unconditional. The truest definition of real love I have ever come to know.

I couldn't trust wholeheartedly because I had made something so simple, oh so hard. And unbelief is what has kept me hindered all these years. All this time I have been praying for healing and restoration. I choose to believe that once I figured out that my soul needed to be restored, I had learned how to be more specific with my prayers. In doing this, His Holy Spirit unlocked a door within me that had been closed since my early childhood.

With all of this, a major release had come. Divine deliverance has allowed me to think differently, believe differently and most importantly, I pray differently. I don't pray out of despair or anguish anymore. I pray with a new mind of knowing, trusting and believing that Jesus loves me. He really is concerned about me. He really is in control of every area of my life and He knows me personally.

He told me one day, "Georgette, I will never leave you, nor forsake you." Today I don't question it because I know that He is always here. Wherever I am, He is! I feel alive more in my spirit than I've ever felt in my entire life. It is so beautiful. I didn't realize how consumed I was until the Holy Spirit freed me and released me.

You too can be free, really free on the inside. This definitely has given me a whole new meaning to my relationship with Jesus Christ. I study and meditate on His Word. Praise God and bless His holy name. John says *"So if the Son sets you free, you will be free indeed."* (John 8:36) Jesus loves you! *"They overcome him by the blood of the lamb and by the word of their testimony."* (Revelation 12:11a)

Chapter 11

Different Voices

Chaplain Yong Hui McDonald

1. The voice

I struggled with thoughts of despair for a long time while our family was suffering from our father's alcoholism and abusive attitudes and behaviors. After my sister died in a tragic car accident, I was deeply depressed and bedridden and suffered from nightmares. My mother told me to read the Bible.

I started reading the Bible and realized that I was a sinner. I was in deep remorse and asked God to forgive me. Something happened right after that. I experienced overwhelming peace which I never had experienced before. I knew then God had forgiven me.

The Bible gave me answers to many questions I had. It gave me direction and hope which I didn't have before. It also has given me the tools to recognize what I need to watch for and what I need to pursue.

In the book of *Romans 12:1-2*, Paul talked about how we need to be transformed by the renewing of our mind. How can I do that? In one area I learned that I could change my mind by continuously reading the Bible and find hope and purpose for my life. I began to understand what kind of blessings God has for me — forgiveness is one of them and eternal salvation is the other. Then there are many more blessings that came to me but I was yet to discover these blessings. They came through struggles and by changing my way of thinking, especially in the areas of recognizing different voices and how to accept or resist them.

As I read the Bible more and more, my nightmares and depressive thoughts slowly started disappearing. The Scripture reading was a good influence for my soul and I found joy in knowing God. I knew God was real. My spirit came alive as I was soaking my heart with the positive thoughts and God's voices through reading His Word. I started attending Bible college because I loved to study the Bible.

2. The voice of doubt

After I started reading the Bible, I had experienced something new. The Bible helped me to recognize my spiritual condition and I experienced peace and joy which I believe was the confirmation from the Lord that I was on the right path. I have no doubt that God loves me and has forgiven me.

Then I started hearing voices that used the Scripture to condemn me saying that God could not forgive me. I was alarmed at first. I didn't know where these voices were coming from. I was hearing them in my mind. I was not just annoyed, but very disturbed by them.

The voices I heard in my mind this time were different. This voice was not convicting my sins which would help me to turn to God for repentance. I knew the feeling of the conviction of sin. When that happens, I understand it comes from the Lord. I will have a deep remorse with a sorrowful heart which leads me to repentance.

These voices though were lying to make me doubt

God's forgiveness. The voices got louder especially when I tried to read the Bible. I began to recognize the spiritual battle inside of me. These voices didn't give me peace but turmoil. There was something besides God which was trying to disturb the peace I found in God.

I didn't think God would do that, so I figured that it must be the devil who tried to discourage me. This experience taught me that the devil can twist the Bible to make me doubt God's grace. I cried out to God for His mercy and I found peace.

I was learning something new. If I would have accepted these voices without reflecting on how much God loves and forgives me, then I would have stopped reading the Bible thinking He cannot forgive me. I began to recognize that the enemy, the devil, was using the Scripture to discourage me from reading the Bible.

Up to that time, I had no idea that the devil would twist the Bible to make me stay away from the Lord, and also try to discourage me from reading the Bible. I knew what to do to win this battle. Whenever the voices would tell me that God cannot forgive me, I fought it with many Scriptures He does forgive me. The following Scriptures helped me a lot in this battle.

"Therefore, there is now no condemnation for those who are in Christ Jesus, because through Christ Jesus the law of the Spirit of life set me free from the law of sin and death. For what the law was powerless to do in that it was weakened by the sinful nature, God did by sending his own Son in the likeness of sinful man to be a sin offering. And so he condemned sin in sinful man, in order that the righteous requirements of the law might be fully met in us, who do not live according to the sinful nature but according to the Spirit." (Romans 8:1-3) "God made

you alive with Christ. He forgave us all our sins, having canceled the written code, with its regulations, that was against us and that stood opposed to us; he took it away, nailing it to the cross." (Colossians 2:13b-14)

I was forgiven not because I was righteous, but because of what Jesus had done for me on the cross. I was forgiven because I repented and asked God to forgive me. The voices didn't want to give up and kept coming back. I don't remember hearing condemning voices before I had my conversion experiences. I heard them after I had conversion experiences. I believe the devil really didn't care when I was not saved because I was living in sin and didn't even recognize it anyway. But after I realized that I was a sinner and forgiven by God, the devil didn't want to lose the ground of all the lies that he was feeding me. So, he tried hard to keep the ground by trying to convince me that God cannot forgive me.

I would apply the Scriptures how God has forgiven me whenever I heard the condemning voice, then the voices stopped. I found victory in that area. I experienced the power of the Scripture because these condemning voices eventually stopped completely.

Because of this experience, I understood how some Christians suffer from tormenting voices that condemn them to the point that they feel God cannot forgive them or God cannot love them because of their sin.

Many years later, when I was working as an intern chaplain at Denver Women's Correctional Facility, I learned that many Christians suffer from these condemning voices more so than non-Christians. These people believed that Jesus died on the cross for their sins, but they hear these bad voices which torment them.

I started teaching a "Forgiveness" class and was able to help others learn how to forgive themselves and others with the help of the Scriptures and the Holy Spirit's healing power. If I didn't go through struggles myself, I couldn't have understood what these people were going through but I understood exactly what they were struggling with. They were tormented by spirits which told them that God cannot forgive them.

Many who came to the class learned how to forgive others and themselves. I know God can do it because He has helped me to be released from the accusing voices.

3. Finding answers

Even though I have gained peace from accusing voices, I still suffered from much turmoil in my mind. Why didn't I have complete freedom in my mind? Why did I struggle so much in my mind with negative and critical voices even after I became a Christian? I had no idea how to sort them out or learn how to deal with different voices to find peace. I thought what I was going through was a normal life. I thought everyone was always in turmoil like me all the time. I was wrong. I just had to learn how to control my mind from different voices, but I didn't know that at the time.

The answer came when I started reading Watchman Nee's book, *Spiritual Man*. In his book, he explained how our mind is a spiritual battlefield. We hear different voices in our mind including the devil's voice and the Holy Spirit's voice.

This was revolutionary to me. No one else told me or taught me or even gave me a hint that what I was hearing in my mind was not always my own thoughts. This book gave me more spiritual insights on why I was still struggling in my mind and taught me to examine what I heard in my mind.

The reason I had so much struggle in my mind was that I was accepting the good voices of the Bible while I was also accepting bad voices without realizing it. As long as I accepted bad voices as my thoughts, I couldn't have peace. I had to learn how to control my thoughts instead of accepting everything as my thoughts. That was the beginning of the healing of my mind.

As I paid attention to the voices and thoughts I was hearing in my mind, I realized how many bad voices I had accepted for so long. The Bible gave me good thoughts, but until I learned to resist the bad thoughts and voices I heard, I was crippled in my spiritual walk with the Lord. As long as I accepted bad voices as my thoughts, the good voice from the Bible had limits.

I also learned a very important lesson from his book. These bad voices do not leave unless I recognize them and resist them. I had lots of work to do to get rid of all the negative thoughts that were affecting my mind and made me see life negatively. In those days, my mind was not clear. I felt like my mind was clouded.

I started changing my attitude and thought process according to the Bible and resisting anything that was contrary to the Bible. I was delivered from the thoughts of despair and depression.

4. Forgiveness

Another insight I gained through understanding these thoughts was that as long as I live in sin, I am not free from bad voices. I struggled to forgive my father for so long. I was praying everyday, "God, please forgive me. I cannot forgive my father. I need you to help me. I cannot love my father." As long as I was seeing my father's abusive behaviors and hearing his critical, hurtful words, I had a difficult time forgiving my father. At the funeral God helped me to understand my father's love and I was able to forgive my father. This helped me to let go of bitterness.

5. The voices of distraction

I developed a strategy of how to fight bad voices. I fight bad voices with Scripture and rebuke them by saying, "In the name of Jesus, leave from me."

After I learned to fight bad voices, I learned that not only bad voices can try to affect my mind by talking to me in my mind, but also in my dreams.

This happened when I tried to fast for three days. I heard the bad voices of evil spirits in my dream that tried to distract me from what I was trying to do.

Also, I heard bad voices when I was going through difficult times. A voice told me to run into a car and kill myself than my problems would end. If I didn't realize that the different voices I hear are not all my thoughts, I could have assumed that these were my thoughts. But, I understood where it came from immediately. Problems in life are a sign that we are still alive and with God's wisdom, we can learn to handle seemingly impossible situations. Just having problems doesn't mean we have to kill ourselves. This was a bad voice from the devil and I rebuked him in the name of Jesus.

Other times when I was flooded with tears of

disappointment and discouragement, I was only thinking about what others couldn't give me. I was immersed in self-pity. While I was crying, I suddenly heard a screaming voice from the back. It was an audible voice of the person that I was having a problem with.

I knew this voice was not from anyone but the demons who tried to confuse me and make me more angry with this person. I was holding resentment and I opened the door to the bad voices. I immediately was on my knees and I confessed my sin, "Forgive me Lord, I forgive, bless and pray for this person." This stopped my tears and I understood how bad voices can hurt me and lead me to hate. I was free from bitterness and found peace. I am continuously learning how to resist bad voices and I recognize how to resist them before I accept them as my own.

6. What else was still missing?

I learned how to resist bad thoughts which were not my thoughts. Yet, at this point in my life, I didn't realize that I was also hearing good voices from God. Therefore, I didn't pay any attention to His voice.

This idea of following good voices came later after I started hearing God calling me to preach and to start a full time ministry. He also started teaching me how to wait and listen. As I reflect, God has been speaking to me through many different ways but I didn't realize that He was speaking to me.

Why didn't I pay attention to good voices? There are many reasons. The first reason is because the churches I attended didn't teach me that God speaks to our heart with good voices and never taught me to resist bad voices. This opened the door to just accept whatever comes to my mind and I thought all my thoughts and voices I heard in my mind are my own thoughts.

Second, I thought God would speak to us only in audible voices like human beings. Thus, I ignored good voices or thoughts in my mind which were from the Lord.

Third, I didn't know that God has many languages. This narrow perception and understanding didn't help me to recognize God's voice for a long time.

I am thankful that the Lord has taught me to listen and wait so I could hear Him. In fact, when I asked the Lord what my calling is, He said, "listening and being a cheerleader for Jesus." This makes perfect sense to me. Listening to God's voices has become a high priority in my life.

7. Writing

I heard God speaking to my heart twice to preach but I didn't want to go into the ministry so I wrote a book, *Moment by Moment* and I thought I was done with the Lord's work.

The day I finished the book, God spoke to me, "Go and tell others Jesus died for their sins and God has forgiven them." The voice was so loud that I could almost see the words with my eyes, but it was not an audible voice. I was hearing it in my spirit. I wasn't ready to commit myself to serve God.

The Holy Spirit started giving me different assignments. I knew the small voice I was hearing in my mind wasn't mine. I couldn't have thought about those things.

They were all good voices and directing me to grow

spiritually and that's how I knew that they came from the Holy Spirit. They didn't come at once but one at a time in the following order: 1) Pray ten percent of your time everyday, like tithing. 2) Read one gospel out loud everyday for a year. 3) Don't just talk to God, but listen to God in silence.

I tried to follow those and I finally realized that Jesus wanted my love, devotion, and for me to serve Him. There is more to it. While I was praying, I learned to listen to God's voice more than anything.

While I was writing *Journey With Jesus*, Jesus convinced me why I need to care for others who are hurting and are in need of Christ's healing presence. I realized that what I needed to do was just to obey and the Holy Spirit will be the one who helps me in my ministry. My heart was changed by God's grace and His persistent calling.

8. Blessings

I have been so blessed since I started following good voices — the Holy Spirit's voice. My ministry has been a blessing for me. I have been to the mountain tops many times. I have seen people transformed in my ministry by the power of the Holy Spirit. The Holy Spirit has convinced me that God can do so much more than what I think or imagine. I am thankful that God has taught me to listen to Him and obey.

The result of obeying the small voice is happiness, fulfillment and joy. Following the good voice has become a very important practice. I listen whenever I can. I listen more than talking to God. I limit what I hear from the outside like watching TV, reading books and even listening to good music.

I have learned to focus on important matters in life

which is to focus my heart on my Lord Jesus, to love and adore Him in my daily practice, and focus on the ministry which God has given me.

9. Listening

One of the blessings that came through my ministry is my book projects. Without listening to the small voice of the Lord, my book project cannot go anywhere. If I try to write when the Lord is not leading, I end up putting it away sooner or later. Even if it may be a good idea, the Lord would not let me go forward. I feel the resistance on the Holy Spirit's part so I have to follow His leading. This book is a good example of it.

After I started my prison ministry, if someone would have asked me what I wanted to write, it was this book. Many people told me how to listen to God's voice and they are willing to learn, but they needed some direction on how to listen. God wouldn't let me finish this book. I don't know how many times I went back to write this book but still the Lord wouldn't let me finish it. I felt stuck. In the mean time the Lord led me to write other books which I never intended to write.

This book was eighty percent ready in the early part of 2011. I was hoping to finish it, but the Lord would not let me and He kept giving me other book assignments. At the same time, He told me the way I was writing would only help ten percent of people. He wanted me to rewrite so that anyone can understand. That meant I needed to do extensive rewriting, but He was not giving me any instructions on how to go forward.

One day I was talking with a friend and she told

me she wanted to learn how to listen to God's voice. I printed my rough draft and gave it to her. About three months later, she called me and asked me when I would finish my book. She offered to help me edit because my rough draft helped her to recognize God's voice.

That encouraged me. I started writing this book again and hoped that God would let me finish. Amazingly, the Lord started directing me to complete this book.

If I were to write any book, this was one book I wanted to write because recognizing different voices, listening and following God's voice changed my life. I can see the transformation in my life after I started obeying the Lord's voice in the following areas:

(1) My relationship with Jesus grew because now I know He is always listening to my heart and prayers. I used to treat Jesus as someone who lived far away and now I treat Him like He is in my living room with the Holy Spirit. Father God is looking down and smiling when I finally learned to recognize that I am here to love Jesus and follow the Holy Spirit's lead in my ministry. I have a clear direction in life as to what I should do to please the Lord.

(2) I have confidence that if I need answers to some spiritual questions, the Lord will give me the answer. He is more than willing to teach me so I can focus on important things in life instead of being weighed down by everyday life problems.

(3) He has given me focus to serve in the areas He wants me to serve. Writing books was not my idea but the Holy Spirit has been guiding me into my book ministry. He is precise on what He wants me to do so I

can be effective and not waste my time or the life that God has given me.

(4) I have learned to trust my own small voice over the years and I don't have the desire to seek out others' guidance unless the Holy Spirit guides me to do it. This gives me comfort knowing that He knows what is best for me and He will guide me if I need others' help.

(5) When I have any problems, I used to make my own decisions on how to solve them. As I look back, I wasted lots of time trying to understand the big picture with my own wisdom and I wasn't able to see it. But since I started recognizing God's voice, I ask Him for understanding and how I should solve the problems. God already knows what I am going through and all I have to do is ask Him instead of trying to guess. This has helped me not to waste my time or energy on something that I shouldn't. I learned that the more I ask, the more I receive God's wisdom and guidance.

10. Leading

What am I hearing from the Lord these days? The Lord has been speaking to me through the Scriptures about how God saw David. It says, *"After removing Saul, he made David their king. He testified concerning him: 'I have found David son of Jesse a man after my own heart; he will do everything I want him to do.'"(Acts 13:22)*

This Scripture is telling me that if my heart is after God's own heart, I will be able to do what He wants me to do. I used to struggle when God asked me to do something because I had my own ideas and plans for my life. I decided that understanding God's heart is the thing that I should pursue so I can do everything God wants me to do in my life.

Prayer: "Dear Lord Jesus, help me to have your heart so I will be able to do what you want me to do. Help me to know your will for my life and guide me so I will listen to and obey the Holy Spirit. Let my love grow like a rose in your garden. I give you praise for helping me finish this book. In Jesus' name I pray. Amen."

Chapter 12: An Invitation

1. An Invitation to Accept Christ

Do you have an empty heart that cannot be filled with anyone or anything? God can fill your empty heart with His love and forgiveness. Do you feel your life has no meaning, no direction, no purpose, and that you don't know where to turn to find the answers? It's time to turn to God. That's the only way you can understand the meaning and purpose of your life. You will find a direction that will lead you to fulfillment and joy. Is your heart broken and hurting? Do you not know how to experience healing? Until we meet Christ in our hearts, we cannot find the peace and healing that God can provide. Jesus can help heal your broken heart. If you don't have a relationship with Christ, this is an opportunity for you to accept Jesus into your heart so you can be saved and experience peace and healing from God. Here is a prayer if you are ready to accept Jesus:

"Dear Jesus, I surrender my life and everything to you. I give you all my pain, fear, regret, resentment, anger, worry, and concerns that overwhelm me. I am a sinner. I need your forgiveness. Please come into my heart and my life and forgive all my sins. I believe that you died for my sins and that you have plans for my life. Please heal my broken heart and bless me with your peace and joy. Help me to cleanse my life so I can live a godly life. Help me to understand your plans for my life and help me to obey you. Fill me with the Holy Spirit, and guide me so I can follow your way. I pray this in Jesus' name. Amen."

2. An Invitation for Transformation Project Prison Ministry (TPPM).

Chaplain Yong Hui V. McDonald has been in prison ministry since 1999. She started working as a chaplain at Adams County Detention Facility (ACDF) in Brighton, Colorado, in 2003. She started the Transformation Project Prison Ministry (TPPM) in 2005 in an effort to bring spiritually nurturing books to the inmates at the facility because the chaplains' office had a shortage of inspirational books. In the process, *Maximum Saints* books and DVDs were produced by ACDF inmates for other inmates.

The *Maximum Saints* books and DVDs project provide the ACDF incarcerated saints an opportunity to put their writing and artistic skills to use to provide hope, peace, restoration, and healing. It also gives spiritual support to incarcerated people, the homeless, as well as to interested persons outside the prisons.

Maximum Saints are not necessarily classified as maximum security inmates; they are called Maximum Saints because they are using their gifts to the maximum to help others.

TPPM is committed to help those who are spiritually hungry and need Christ's message. Within six years, TPPM has produced eight English books, two Spanish books and four DVDs. That's God's grace.

"One Million Dream Project"

Books and DVDs produced by TPPM are distributed in jails, prisons, and homeless shelters nationwide free of charge. This is made possible by grants and donations. America has 2.3 million people incarcerated, the largest prison population in the world, and there is a great shortage of inspirational books in many jails and prisons.

In 2010, TPPM board decided to expand the ministry goal, and started "One Million Dream Project." TPPM decided to raise enough funds to distribute one million copies of each book TPPM produces to prisoners and homeless people. I ask you to pray for this project so God can help TPPM reach out to those who cannot speak for themselves but are in need of spiritual guidance from the Lord.

TPPM is a 501(c)(3) nonprofit organization so your donation is 100% tax deductible. If you would like to be a partner in this very important mission of bringing transformation through the message of Christ in prisons and homeless shelters or want to know more about this project, go to the website: www.maximumsaints.org. You can donate online or you can write a check to: Transformation Project Prison Ministry and send it to the following address:

Transformation Project Prison Ministry
5209 Montview Boulevard
Denver, CO 80207

Website: www.maximumsaints.org
Facebook: http://tinyurl.com/yhhcp5g
Email: maximumsaints@maximumsaints.org

3. How to Purchase *Maximum Saints Books*.

This is for individuals who would like to purchase or send a copy of *Maximum Saints* books to their incarcerated family. TPPM receives lots of requests for individual distribution but we only distribute them through chaplains. All the proceeds from *Maximum Saints* will go to TPPM to distribute more free books and DVDs to prisons and homeless shelters. To find out more about purchasing *Maximum Saints* books, check our website: www.maximumsaints.org.

The following books are available:

Book One: *Maximum Saints Never Hide in the Dark*
Book Two: *Maximum Saints Make No Little Plans*
Book Three: *Maximum Saints Dream*
Book Four: *Maximum Saints Forgive*
Book Five: *Maximum Saints All Things Are Possible*

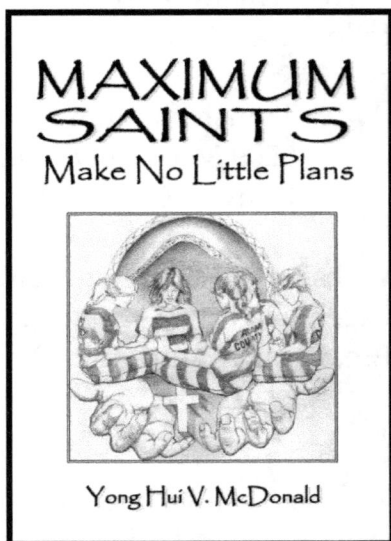

MAXIMUM SAINTS DREAM

Yong Hui V. McDonald

MAXIMUM SAINTS FORGIVE

Yong Hui V. McDonald

MAXIMUM SAINTS
All Things Are Possible

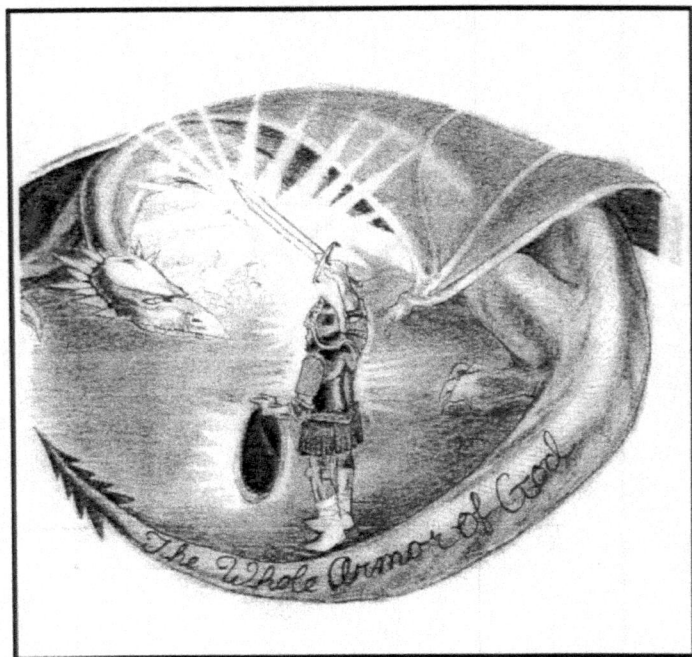

The Whole Armor of God

Yong Hui V. McDonald

ABOUT THE AUTHOR

Yong Hui V. McDonald, also known as Vescinda McDonald, is a chaplain at Adams County Detention Facility, certified American Correctional Chaplain, spiritual director and on-call hospital chaplain. She founded the Transformation Project Prison Ministry (TPPM) in 2005 and founded GriefPathway Ventures, LLC, in 2010 to help others learn how to process grief and healing. She also is the founder of Veterans Twofish Foundation, a 501(c)(3) non-profit, in 2011, to provide inspirational resources to veterans..

Education:
- Multnomah Bible College, B.A.B.E. (1984)
- Iliff School of Theology, Master of Divinity (2002)
- The Samaritan Counseling & Educational Center, Clinical Pastoral Education (CPE) (2002)
- Rocky Mountain Pastoral Care and Training Center (CPE) (2003)
- Vincentian Center Spirituality and Work, Formation Program for Spiritual Directors (2004)
- Rocky Mountain Pastoral Care and Training Center (CPE), Recovery of Soul: Spiritual Care Ministry Training (2011)

Books and Audio Books by Yong Hui V. McDonald:
- *Moment by Moment*
- *Journey With Jesus, Visions, Dreams, Meditations & Reflections*
- *Dancing in the Sky, A Story of Hope for Grieving Hearts*
- *Twisted Logic, The Shadow of Suicide*
- *Twisted Logic, The Window of Depression*

- *Dreams & Interpretations, Healing from Nightmares*
- *I Was The Mountain, In Search of Faith & Revival*
- *The Ultimate Parenting Guide, How to Enjoy Peaceful Parenting and Joyful Children*
- *Prisoners Victory Parade, Extraordinary Stories of Maximum Saints & Former Prisoners*
- *Four Voices, How They Affect Our Mind: How to Overcome Self-Destructive Voices and Hear the Nurturing Voice of God*
- *Tornadoes, Grief, Loss, Trauma, and PTSD: Tornadoes, Lessons and Teachings – The TLT Model for Healing*
- Compiled and published five *Maximum Saints* books under the Transformation Project Prison Ministry.

DVDs produced by Yong Hui:
- *Dancing in The Sky, Mismatched Shoes*
- *Tears of The Dragonfly, Suicide and Suicide Prevention (CD* is also available*)*

Spanish books produced by Yong Hui:
- *Twisted Logic, The Shadow of Suicide*
- *Journey With Jesus, Visions, Dreams, Meditations & Reflections*

GriefPathway Ventures, LLC
P.O. Box 220
Brighton, CO 80601
Website: www.griefpathway.com
Email: griefpwv@gmail.com

Veterans Twofish Foundation

Veterans Twofish Foundation
P.O. Box 220 Brighton, CO 80601
Website: veteranstwofish.org